from Bill

3 - John - 2

I'm All SHOOK UP

EVANGELIST

BILL DUNN

Published by
Maurice Wylie Media
Your Christian Book Publisher

Publisher's statement: Throughout this book the love for our God is such that whenever we refer to Him we honour with capitals. On the other hand, when referring to the devil, we refuse to acknowledge him with any honour to the point of violating grammatical rule and withholding capitalisation.

Dedication

There are those to whom I shall ever be grateful, and it is to them that I dedicate this book. My late wife Iris, the love of my life who received her home call to heaven in 2016. This was a deep valley I had to walk through with my broken heart.

Our sons Paul and Jonathan who bring me great joy and delight every day, while along with their wives, Gail and Annette, keep reminding me that I don't have to be a super-hero and wear spandex tights and a cape, I just need to be *Dad*.

Both boys came to faith in Jesus when they were young, Paul at five years of age and Jonathan at six.

Jonathan came to Jesus through his older brother Paul who started preaching when he was around six years of age. While I was at Bible college and Iris living with my mum and out at work, my mum would have small gospel meetings every Thursday when some of her friends met for tea and cakes. After tea mum would set up a little fireguard for Paul, who got his ukulele and lead them in choruses, then get his Bible and preach acting out what he had watched his me do in church.

Paul recorded himself preaching about The Coming Jesus, on a tape recorder. Unknown to us all six-year-old Jonathan got hold of the tape and played it back and forth and came to his mum and said, "I want to be saved."

While pastoring a church in Banbridge in Northern Ireland, one night watching a broadcast on the television about brain surgery, well in truth Iris was, I couldn't watch it. I went to the study to read. Jonathan was sitting watching it with his mum and then the program was over, he came to me in the study and said, "Daddy, I want to be a brain surgeon." I just knew there was one in the Dunn family somewhere, this must be him. "That's good son," I replied.

The Banbridge grew in number as people were getting saved and joining the church. One family in particular named McCracken, drove the Maine Minerals delivering the lemonade around the shops and homes.

Once a week the McCracken's would call at our home with fizzy drinks. Jonathan was about seven years of age. One afternoon Jonathan arrived home from school ands he said, "Dad, can I talk to you? I don't want to be a brain surgeon; I want to be a lemonade man."

Today Paul pastors the Elim Church in Ballymena, Northern Ireland, and Jonathan works in a large company that sells lemonade plus other items. Both boys got their dream.

I am thankful for a wonderful mum…

Contents

Contact **164**

Acknowledgements

I would like to express my thanks to each and every one who has encouraged me and helped me to write this book, this includes Pastor Eric McComb, who wrote the foreword, to those who have written an endorsement, to Maurice Wylie Media team for putting up with me and giving me something special in this book.

We all arrive on this planet not knowing where we came from, wondering why we are here and asking what the future holds. This is my journey through the joys and tears, the ups and downs of life, in this crazy mixed-up world and the lessons I have learnt along the way.

Now, after many years of promising so many I would write this book, I have finally got round to it. I'm writing with you in mind, in the hope that you will understand your life is not a biological mistake, in the hope that you will realise that you have been put on this planet for a purpose, even if that purpose has been to push me to write this story of God's grace in my life and His dealings with me.

Endorsements

The story of Bill Dunn's life is one of dramatic transformation followed by consistent obedience to the voice of God.

It is a remarkable account of how God intervened powerfully in the life of a young musician and singer who was totally immersed in the Irish show-band and rock and roll scene of the 1960s.

Upon leaving that world behind, Bill set out on a path that would see his God-given talents used for a different and greater cause.

What began with simply sharing the story of his life-changing encounter would lead to theological training, years of local church ministry, itinerant evangelistic preaching, the recording of fourteen Christian albums, and involvement in radio and television ministry.

This astonishing story recounting fifty-seven years of ministry and evangelistic preaching, which took Bill from the shores of Northern Ireland to England, Scotland, America, Canada, Africa, the Republic of Ireland and back to his native home is a gripping account of God leading and one man's passion to share the *good news*.

Pastor Edwin Michael
Superintendent of the Elim Church in Ireland.

My life was impacted by Bill Dunn long before I met him. As a young Christian, at the beginning of the 1980's, someone gave me a cassette tape of Bill's challenging the lyrics of contemporary songs and their influence on the listener, exposing back-tracking, sometime referred to as "backwards-masking." Whether or not I agreed with all that he said he was the first person to make me think of the importance of words with music and their potential power for good or ill. We became ministerial colleagues and I have admired his completely positive expectation of God's goodness being manifest in lives of others.

Phil Hills, Vice President, Global Teen Challenge.

Bill Dunn is not just a name that is known far and wide in the evangelical world — it's more than that. It's a name that is precious to us as a family. On March 16, 1986, Bill pointed my wife Tracy to Christ and a few months later he baptised her by immersion. How more important could the man be to us than that.

I've known Bill for many years and I have had him share in most of the gospel missions that I have conducted and had him preach several times at the Tabernacle. He's the wee man with a big heart. A big heart for God. A big heart for the gospel and big heart for those who know not Christ.

It is my privilege to be invited to write this endorsement to his book. One thing you will discover; he is an ordinary man, with an extraordinary message, which he shares with ordinary people to bring hope and blessing to all who hear him.

Another thing; no matter what battle you face in life, it's Bill who reminds us, *Don't give up, you're on the brink of a miracle.*

Pastor George McConnell
Kilkeel Baptist Tabernacle, Northern Ireland.

I first met Bill in 1967, in The Net, a Christian coffee bar in Belfast's Ormeau Road. He was singing in a gospel group he had formed named *The Evangels* and it was easy to see that he was destined for greater things.

A couple of years later Bill embarked on a solo ministry not only ministering in song but a preaching ministry as well. With great sincerity and passion the Word was preached and sung from a heart full of love for God and for the lives of all who came to listen.

Bill also had the great privilege of ministering through his own gospel music programme which reached millions across Europe on the Sky satellite television platform and also through a weekly radio broadcast for UCB Ireland.

Over the years Bill has recorded several gospel music albums, many of these tracks I featured over the years on my *Gospel Time* programme on Downtown Radio.

As you read the chapters of this book you will see the heart of a man not only with a great sense of humour but a sincere heart sold out to his Saviour, Jesus Christ. A man who wants to reach the lonely, the least, the lost and see their lives transformed to the glory of His Lord.

Ronnie Morrison
The Morrison's Gospel Group and former producer/presenter at Downtown Radio, Northern Ireland.

It has been my privilege to know Pastor Bill Dunn from shortly after his conversion to Christ in the 1960s. We were both young men seeking to serve the Lord by witnessing, singing and testifying at the great open-air meetings in the city of Belfast.

Over the past years, I have found Bill to be a faithful preacher and pastor, a faithful family man and a true servant of God.

After walking away from a life touring as a rock singer and musician, he dedicated all his talents to the furtherance of the Gospel of Christ and threw himself wholeheartedly into the work of God and employed his gifts to sing and preach the Word of God.

I count it a great joy to have been able to share with him in many gospel missions, meetings, evenings of praise and Christian fellowships, without forgetting a number of protests and witness for the Crown rights of King Jesus and uphold His Word and the Lord's Day.

I am sure that this book will be a blessing and a benefit to all who read it, an encouragement to the saints of God and a challenge to the unsaved.

Rev. Dr Fred Greenfield
Free Presbyterian Church of Ulster.

Pastor Bill Dunn's ministry has stood the test of time. He continues to share the gospel at every opportunity, with a willing spirit and unending enthusiasm to share the Lord's love for him and his love for the Lord. It is this rescuing love for His Saviour Jesus that has permeated his life and ministry and forms the bedrock of this unfolding story.

I first met Bill while pastoring the Elim church at Caledon when he came by invitation to hold an evangelistic tent crusade on the church grounds.

Over the years, Bill's heartfelt care of people has moved him to raise much needed finance for Elim missions overseas, as well as for the Northern Ireland Children's Hospice.

His commitment, resilience and vision are inspirational. He has never lost the joy of serving the Lord through his gift of preaching and music, even during times of loneliness and grief. This generation of godly servants has much to teach us all.

Rev. Roy Johnston
Irish Missions Director for Elim, Ireland.

Foreword

The 1976 annual ordination service of the Elim Pentecostal Church was held in the prestigious building that is Westminster Chapel, London. There were seventeen ordinands that year, three were from Northern Ireland, Tommy McGuicken, Eric McComb and the author of this book, Pastor Bill Dunn. Quite an occasion for Tommy, Eric and Bill to be ordained in a chapel.

After pastoring in Scotland, Bill returned home with his wife, Iris, and two young sons, Paul and Jonathan, to serve the Lord in Ireland, where he has used his singing gift for the glory of God. Furthermore, he has shown himself to be a preacher with a great evangelistic ministry.

He believes passionately in the message he preaches, and over the years that passion has never waned. His heart beats with enthusiasm, and the arteries have not hardened with age. He has been astute enough to recognise that the style of presenting the gospel can change, but the substance is non-negotiable.

His sermons continue to catch the attention of his audience by communicating the gospel story in a language that everyone understands. The message he preaches addresses the sinful nature of the world in which we live with great simplicity and sincerity.

Drabness and deadness have never been part of Bill's approach to ministry. Instead, he displays vibrancy and a God-centred focus to whatever task he is engaged in. His theme song, *Don't Give Up You're on the Brink of a Miracle* brought encouragement to many a despairing spirit.

Many years ago, I opened the post one morning and there was a card from Bill with the words, "Don't give up you're on the brink of a miracle."

That card was the encouragement I needed that Monday morning to keep my eyes fixed on the Lord, and overcome my faint-heartedness.

For the past fifty years in Elim, and in his time with the Christian Worker's Union, Bill's message has not changed. It's a message of hope to a sinful world and a Christ who died to set us free. He hasn't sought to condense the gospel or alter it to be seeker friendly, but he believes it can stand on its own two feet without human interference.

Ruth and I have counted it a great privilege to serve with Bill and his late wife, Iris. Iris and Bill walked and served together with God, and her promotion to glory, has left a huge void in Bill's life. Iris stood with Bill in the good times, and in those times when ministry was challenging. As a wife and mother, she walked day by day with her Lord, and supported Bill every step of the way.

To all who read this story *I'm All Shook Up,* you will be blessed, encouraged and inspired.

Pastor Eric McComb
Former superintendent of the Elim Pentecostal Church in Ireland.

Introduction

For those of you who don't know me, let me introduce myself. As the endorsements have alluded to, I have spent most of my life ministering around Northern Ireland, a place I am grateful to call home, and further afield.

In using the word ministering I don't mean in the political sense but as a pastor/evangelist in *Church ministry*. I came to have faith in Jesus Christ in my early twenties; it is a ministry that had small beginnings from a little terrace house in East Belfast, and which grew to reach the world.

For many of you who will read this book, like me, there are times when our minds recall those happiest times of our lives, those special childhood years.

Like most boys of my age I was involved in the usual stuff for kids of that era. In the 1950s we played cowboys and Indians, like our heroes in the Saturday morning movie matinee. I loved running around in the forest of Orangefield in Belfast — that was before it was made into a concrete jungle and back then I had no aches in my body. We were crawling through the grass like World War Two commandos, climbing trees like Tarzan, fighting alongside like Jim Bowie and Davy Crockett at the Alamo and raiding the apple orchards along Cyprus Avenue.

I was also the *champion marble player* of Bloomfield, and boasted a large sweetie jar full of glass marbles. Whatever happened to those marbles? There is probably a collector out there willing to pay a lot of money for them.

I was into all that life offered at that time; I joined most of the youth organisations of the day, the Life Boys, the Boy Scouts and the Boy's

Brigade, to name a few. You name it and I was most likely in it. One of my chums chirped, "Hey Dunner, if you wear a skirt they'll let you join the Girls Brigade."

I was in and out of everything and committed to nothing. Even years later when I turned to faith in God, my sister said to Mum, "Just another passing phase our Billy is going through, it won't last."

I did not realise, there was a part of me hungering for more, but wondering what it was. You see, a baby's cry might stop for a little time with a toy rattle but when it's hungry ... the baby will keep crying until the hunger is fed and the baby feels satisfied.

Inside every one of us is a cry of hunger and thirst that nothing of this world seems able to fully satisfy. This is how it was with me, searching for a magic formula that would change my life and open a way that would finally lead me to a deep sense of fulfilment, but it was much later when I realised what that real fulfilment would be.

Throughout the highs and lows of my life, I always found great joy and satisfaction in music. In fact, I can never remember a time when I wasn't around music in some shape or form. Everyone in our family was great singers, Dad, Mum, my older brother Jackie who emigrated to Canada, and my sister Agnes, even the sewing machine was named a *Singer.'*

Speaking of which, as a tribute to my great love of music and the many amazing songs I have sung, I have used song titles throughout the book ... how music worked for me like a soothing therapy for my emotions. I discovered music could lift your spirit when you are feeling down, like an invisible pair of hands wrapping themselves around you in those dark moments when memories of the past come rushing in, or you experience the apprehension of a sudden jolt from an unwelcome situation.

When we are stressed, the surge of negative emotions can be overwhelming. It's in those moments that we reach out for something. Some turn to drugs, alcohol, or sex, many others go shopping. In my case, before I came to believe in Jesus Christ it was music. Songs such as *You'll Never Walk Alone,* Jerry and the Pacemakers. *Sweet Caroline,* Neil Diamond. *Dancing Queen,* Abba. *It's Now or Never,* Elvis, are but a few that got me round the twists and turns on the journey of life.

I truly believe that life is like a book we are writing every day, the past is a history full of memories good and bad, while the future is a series of brilliant opportunities disguised as impossible situations.

My mother used to say, "There are three sides to every story. There's yours, Billy, there's mine, and there is God's. God knows more about us than we do about ourselves, He can fix it."

As I share my life story in the pages of this book, I have learnt that as time passes, the disappointments in life don't cancel God's assignments for my life. The moment I handed my life over to God and began doing it His way, He has done more with it than I could ever have done.

God's singer of songs and writer of prose, David King of Israel expresses this in Psalm 139:16–17 NIV, *"Your eyes saw my unformed body; all the days of my life ordained for me were written in your book before one of them came to be. How precious to me are your thoughts, God. How vast are the sum of them."* Or, "How amazing are your thoughts concerning me."

Chapter 1

"Still Haven't Found What I'm Looking For ..."

(Song written by Bono)

May 1943 — the date the stork dropped me off at the Belfast Royal Victoria Hospital is all very vague. But from what my parents told me and what I read in history books and TV documentaries of that time; Hitler was waging a war across Europe when I was born, and he knocked on the doors of the United Kingdom for several years.

A number of people say they don't believe in God; there is no evidence He walks the earth because they have never seen Him. They hear people talk about Him and read stories of Him in a book called the Bible, but they have never met Him, so they conclude God doesn't exist. In my lifetime I never saw or met Hitler, but I heard people talk about him and have read about him in history books, so I conclude that he at one time walked the earth. In fact, consider how many witnesses he had to confirm he existed?

John and Catherine Dunn, with their newborn baby in their arms, along with my older brother Jackie and sister Agnes had to flee, like many others for safety to Orangefield, a forest situated at the top of the Bloomfield Road in Belfast. This was to escape the bombing of the Belfast Rope Works that was just a few yards away from the row of little terrace houses in Greenville Street where we lived.

That same month, RAF Bomber Command Squadron 617 retaliated and gave Hitler and his cohorts a thrashing when they smashed the dams of the Ruhr Valley in Germany by using the revolutionary *Bouncing Bomb*. Later, this incident was made into a British war movie named *The Dam Busters*.

The only memory I have of World War Two was after it ended, when at the age of five as I held my sister's hand, we watched a crane with a large metal ball attached as it knocked down the air-raid shelters at the end of our street and the surrounding streets that lined Ravenscroft and Bloomfield Avenue.

I was christened, William Wilson Dunn in the parish of St Donard's Church of Ireland in the Bloomfield district in East Belfast. The name William Wilson was given to me because of an uncle who was affectionately known as Uncle Willie. If he had lived into my teenage years, I would most likely have been a full-time soccer player rather than a musician. I think he had high hopes that one day I would lead his favourite soccer team, Glentoran onto the Oval pitch wearing the green shirt. Every Saturday he taught me what he knew about kicking and to dribble a ball like Sir Stanley Matthews, who played for Stoke City and Blackpool. But his dream of me playing for Glentoran came to an abrupt end when one morning on his way to work he suffered a heart attack and died.

Although times were hard back then, I had a happy childhood even though I was born with a health problem — chronic bronchitis, which made breathing difficult at times. We lived in a damp terrace house, which was known as a *kitchen house,* because it had only two rooms upstairs and two down, and a small kitchen that exacerbated the problem.

I often smile when I hear people refer to those times as the *good old days*. Unlike today, there was no double glazing on the windows and doors or central heating, or carpet on the floor. There was oil-cloth that was sometimes covered by a large mat. An open fire that burnt coal and anything else heated the house. There was no indoor bathroom such as we have today. In all the small houses where we lived the bath hung on a nail in the backyard and the toilet was outside. I can tell you in winter time you didn't sit out there and read a newspaper or a book for long.

Today the world has become a neighbourhood without being a brotherhood, but back then neighbours pulled together to support one another. Like wee Mrs Silcock, who lived a few doors up the street and often asked my mum for the loan of some sugar or milk until her husband's pay-day on Friday.

The majority of the families living in the street were good, hard-working neighbours. Of course, in every community, the same as today, there are usually one or two who never seem to be able to sort out their domestic problems.

There was one family that I recall who were always fighting among themselves; for their own health and safety the neighbours knew not to get involved.

One afternoon on my way home from school as I got near their house I heard them shouting. There was the sound of smashed glass as a dartboard flew out of the window and landed at my feet. I hurried past their house. I continued to watch but pretended I wasn't so I could get past before darts followed the dartboard.

Then there was my Aunt Nan who lived in Steen's Row off Beersbridge Road, a row of small terrace houses with eight on both sides of the street. The street was so narrow it was said that if you ran down the stairs of your house with the front door open you would be running up the stairs of the house on the opposite side of the street. When they finally demolished the old houses there was enough space to build an Elim Church on the plot of land.

After Aunt Nan's husband died of a heart attack she took me into Belfast on Saturdays where she bought me a gift, then treated me to a two course dinner — I loved the apple sponge and custard.

Aunt Nan was a character, a tough Belfast woman who lived on her own and who worked in the Owen O'Cork Mill off Beersbridge Road. She was not the best baker in the province but would try her hand at anything and then get me to test it. She took special pride in her *rock cakes*. "Take your pick Billy," she said to me. They were so hard I would have needed a pick from a building site. But Aunt Nan had a heart of gold, which was often expressed in practical ways towards me. I loved her and wouldn't have hurt her by refusing those *rock cakes*. And besides, I would have been afraid to.

We live in a changing world; things never remain the same for long. It has been called, *the throw-away generation.* Why is it we are surprised and horrified to hear David Attenborough talk about there being too much junk in the world that threatens us with climate change? Today, many are willing to put up with the stress and pressures of modern-day living that rob them of peace and contentment for the price of a modern-day lifestyle.

We get caught up in the *must haves* of the 21st century, the latest mobile phone, a larger television, a new car at the door paid for by monthly instalments over three or four years, and, of course, a foreign holiday each year, while deep down inside there's an emptiness these things cannot fill nor will ever fully satisfy, as we always hope that things might get better. Jesus said, *"Seek first the Kingdom of God above all else, and live righteously, and He will give you everything you need"* Matthew 6:33, NLT.

Although life was much simpler back then than it is today, I haven't met anyone recently who wants to go back to those so-called *good old days*. They are willing to put up with the stress and anxiety of modern-day living to have the modern-day things. Little wonder we hear so much talk about mental illness.

Along with my older brother Jackie and sister Agnes, Greenville Street number sixteen was more than a house where we lived, it was a home where I felt safe in my own space because we had parents who loved us and worked hard to provide for us.

There were two schools near to where we lived, Elmgrove Primary off Beersbridge Road and Bloomfield Primary in East Bread Street. My older brother Jackie and sister Agnes and I were sent to Bloomfield. Our parents made this choice because it was nearer to home and less dangerous for us to walk to school. Unlike Elmgrove, which today is still situated on the bend of a busy road, one of the main arteries into Belfast.

Bill and his parents John and Catherine Dunn

Primary school never made any impression on me, nor did it build into me aspirations for my future. It was not the teacher's fault; it was probably because I was but a child and too young to understand the importance of the big world that I needed to prepare for. Along with this, I seem to be on an internal search, and as I hadn't found what I was looking for, I became a daydreamer. When I started school, World War Two had ended just a few years earlier, so while the teacher spoke to the class I was doodling and drawing aerial battles of World War Two — the Spitfire and Messerschmitt in conflict during the famous Battle of Britain. This daydreaming and lack of interest followed me into secondary school.

On one occasion, during an afternoon maths class the teacher was giving us homework to be handed in the next day. My mind was far from addition, subtraction and division of numbers, I was thinking about practice with the band later that night. So when the teacher was giving out the homework all I remembered hearing was the numbers three, four, five, six and seven. When I arrived home and opened these pages I gasped. On each page there were four or five equations to do. It took me all afternoon and into the evening to complete the homework.

The next day when I handed in my work the teacher just smiled.

"Not listening again Dunn?" he said.

"What do you mean, sir?" I asked.

"If you had been listening, you would have heard me tell the class, on page three, do equations four, five, six and seven. That's just four items from page three I was asking for."

That incident cured me of daydreaming in class.

I was the youngest in the family. Both my brother and sister were much older than me. When they finished school my brother trained to be a plumber and worked in the Belfast shipyard. Later, when he married Winnie Douglas, they immigrated to Canada where he established a successful plumbing business.

My sister Agnes worked in the Belfast Ropeworks adjacent to where we lived in Greenville Street. After marrying Jackie Ryall, from Dundella Street, she returned to further her studies and emerged into secretarial work. My brother-in-law Jackie, or Jake as we named him, to save any confusion in the family, worked in the building trade but got out of this when he bought a milk delivery run and built it into a lucrative business.

Living and growing up in a city, and Belfast was no different, you had to be street-wise and learn to defend your corner.

Mum and dad were God-fearing people like many back then, not in the evangelical sense of the word, but they made sure their offspring were taught standards in life, rules, morals, and the Ten Commandments. When they went to church I accompanied them.

My mum believed in the laying on of hands, not in the biblical sense of the word but in the practical.

As a boy in primary school I was always told to come straight home from school. I remember the day a number of my young friends from school who lived in Oakdale and Ashdale Streets at the end of Bloomfield Avenue — streets that are no longer there. They lured me away to the back entry of one of their houses and taught me new words that I hadn't heard before.

When I felt a sting on the back of my legs, it was my wee mum. She had come looking for me. In her hand was the leather belt my father had cut into thin strips. That day I learnt to dance like Michael Flatley the whole way back to Greenville Street. It was called the dance of *the Cat of Nine Tales.*

I learnt more from that experience than all my time spent in school. My dad guided me with his eye. He just looked at me and I knew it was time to change my behaviour.

We hear of people today being called heroes, well, my mum and dad were my heroes. They taught me the ethic, "If you want it, work for it and never go into debt, never owe no one anything." And they set us an example. So like other boys of my age I took on a paper round from Monday through to Saturday and delivered newspapers in the streets and avenues around the Upper Newtownards Road and Hollywood Road, Lomond Avenue, Cheviot Avenue, Finvoy Street and many others. My dad was the main bread earner in the house. He was employed in the famous Belfast shipyard as a plumber's helper while Mum was a stay-at-home wife. One night, I remember my brother telling Mum how the plumber had a much easier job than the plumber's helper because he had to carry all the tools in a large bag while he also assisted the plumber.

Unlike today it was not expected for husband and wife to both have a job. It was up to the man to have a job and provide for his family while his wife looked after the home and cared for the children. My grandparents died young, which placed a big responsibility on my Mum's shoulders. As the oldest in the family she took charge of looking after her brother and two sisters, Joe, Beckey and my Aunt Lily. She became like a mum to them.

She never spoke about it to me. I learnt about it after she died and my Aunt Beckey told me the story. There are heroes everywhere, they don't wear capes or receive an academy award or an MBE from the queen. They don't all live in big houses; most likely they are sitting across the room from you drinking a cup of tea. Appreciate them and love them because you won't have them forever.

Until I was twelve and prior to becoming a teenager, I was sent to Sunday School every Sunday afternoon where I had patient Sunday school teachers such as Mr Lamb the Superintendent, Billy Gillespie, Joe Embelton, and others who taught me the scriptures which built into my psyche the need to have God in my life and life-long principals to live by.

As a child I never identified as being a Christian. I believed in the existence of God, but to say I was a bonafide believer would be an exaggeration.

I believe that the influence in our home and the scriptural teaching in those early Sunday School meetings laid the spiritual foundation in my life for the future.

I never at any time took the Lord's name in vain, swore or used foul language, and didn't fall asleep at night until I said my prayers, even when I was intoxicated.

I remember on several occasions coming home drunk after a night out on the town, and staggering up the stairs drunk. As I held on to the bannister rail I recited what is commonly known as The Lord's Prayer.

I never showed disrespect or tried to humiliate someone for their religious views. This could be the reason they found it easy to open a conversation about God and share their faith views with me. They probably thought they had a spellbound listening ear, but unbeknown to them I wasn't interested.

There was one occasion when I was about eighteen years old and a Jehovah's Witness buttonholed me while I was painting a new factory.

At lunchtime he had his New World Translation Bible in his hand and pointed out certain verses to me while the other men sat eating lunch and winking at one another and mumbling under their breath. On the way home, later that day, as I was standing in a bus queue, he was there and he didn't stop talking. The whole experience was embarrassing, but even though I wasn't interested I didn't want to show disrespect to him. At first I thought he was sincere, but I concluded in time that he was wrong in his interpretation of the Bible. Jesus Christ *is* the Son of the living God, and only through Him can we achieve forgiveness of sin and peace with God — not through any religious act or good works of our own.

If a religious act or good-living life style of our own making could bring us peace with God it raises the question, why was it necessary for Jesus Christ to die such a horrible death on a cross? The Bible says, *"Not by works of righteousness which we have done, but according to His mercy He saved us"* Titus 3:5, KJV.

Chapter Two

"It's Been a Hard Day's Night"

(Song written by John Lennon and Paul McCartney)

Growing up in East Belfast in the 1940s/50s was a safe place for children, which was far removed from the Northern Ireland *Troubles*, that kicked off in 1969, and stole the innocence and future prospects of many a teenage boy or girl who later joined a paramilitary organisation. I remember one such man who had done time in prison for terrorism. After his release he was greatly troubled and haunted with memories about his past life. He said to me, "Life is like a tube of toothpaste, all the good gets pushed out, and you can't get it back in."

Time is a gift no one can keep. If it is abused or misused we suffer years of regret. But if time is used wisely we won't be haunted with memories of the past. This was a lesson that I, like others, had to learn.

I was born in the east of Belfast where there is a strong Protestant enclave. I lived under the shadow of the Belfast shipyard where the world's most famous ship *the Titanic* was built and as previously mentioned, the Belfast Rope Works, which at that time was the largest rope-making firm in the world, which filled orders from every corner of the globe.

The people from *Norn Ireland,* that is how we pronounce it in Belfast, are down-to-earth, hard-working people known for their friendliness, humour and candour.

During those dark days of the *Troubles* amid all the bombing, shooting, and the mayhem and madness that was going on, we got on with life as best as we could, and kept the *never give up or give in spirit.* One of the ways we did this was by telling jokes about politicians from both sides of the religious divide. I remember one in particular — when IRA member Martin McGuinness and the other one who said he never was in the IRA Gerry Adams, first entered politics, you never saw them in suits — a shirt and tie and polished shoes, but they always wore big woolly jumpers and jeans. When they came into the limelight and *look at us now* as politicians, they began dressing like business men.

One night in a pub somewhere in Belfast a group of men were talking about Gerry and Martin. During the conversation one of the men said, "And do you see the suits those boys are wearing now, they're Armani suits?"

An old geezer within earshot swallowed his drink, then wiped his lips and interjected, "Ay boys, and it's our money that's paying for them."

Over the years, Belfast and the surrounding area has thrown up a cluster of famous names including the late George Best, the soccer legend regarded as one of the greatest in the beautiful game. Sadly, George followed in his mother's footsteps and became an alcoholic which hastened the end of his life. Then there was the late Billy Bingham MBE, former Northern Ireland football manager who successfully took the national team to two World Cup tournaments. C.S. Lewis, was another famous person, who during his teenage years through to his early twenties, openly confessed to being an atheist, but later rejected atheism and converted to Christianity in 1931. Let's not forget world snooker champion Alex Higgins and founding father of the Special Air Service (SAS), Lieutenant Colonel Robert Blair *Paddy* Mayne, and so many more.

Musically, we have done well too, with *Them,* the rawest R&B band to ever come out of Northern Ireland and storm the world music scene in the 1960s, led by my buddy Van Morrison. We shall talk about that experience later, and how *Van, the man*, the famous little guy from East Belfast and I got on together.

At the age when children are usually doing kid's stuff, I was engaged in singing impersonations of a white American from New York who blackened his face and had great success with hit songs such as, *California Here I Come, Swanne River, April Showers,* and *Climb Upon My Knee Sonny Boy.* With the present political climate and the rise of *Black Lives Matter* which began in July 2013, to blacken one's face as Al Jolson did, to entertain would be seen today as being racist. But Al Jolson was the heart throb of teenagers throughout the 1940s until Frank Sinatra took the crown from him.

After my Aunt Nan's husband, Uncle Willie died, she took me to work parties and Christmas events where wee Billy wore short trousers and his daddy's waistcoat, and with his face blackened he impersonated Al Jolson. People roared with laughter at my performance during those difficult post-war years.

From an early age I wasn't afraid of being involved and getting my hands dirty. The word entrepreneur was never heard back then as often as it is today, but I believe my entrepreneurial spirit enabled me to set up my own business in the hope of making a profit.

Around the age of ten I went to Stewarts on Beersbridge Road, which was a small version of the present-day Tesco and Asda. I asked the manager if he had any empty wooden onion boxes. He gave me quite a few, which I chopped up and made into bundles of sticks, before I went from door to door and sold the lot for a tanner each, (6d) in old money. If you want your dreams to come true you must get out of bed each morning and go to work.

School was not one of my favourite pastimes, the only appeal was the half past three bell. Bloomfield Primary School in East Bread Street, was where I started my education; today the building is used for Sea Cadets. After leaving primary school at the age of twelve, I entered Ashfield Boys Secondary School on Holywood Road.

Around that time the guitar became popular through a new style of music that was sweeping through Britain and Ireland. It was known as *skiffle*. Lonnie Donegan is regarded as the British pop star who invented the skiffle-style while he played the banjo in the Chris Barber Jazz Band. Skiffle wasn't pop music as it is seen today, it was more a mix of country and folk music.

Lonnie Donegan was our idol back then. Little did we know he was a troubled soul. In a television interview he talked about his deep disappointment after the end of a hectic tour throughout the year. Every theatre in the country was full. He thought they had made a colossal amount of money; however, he was informed by his accountant that he only had £1,100.25 in his bank account. Most of it had been taken in tax because his accountant had foolishly put him on *Pay As You Earn*.

He admitted to often being lonely as he stumbled through life and watched out for the cracks in the pavement. He was asked if he believed in a *Higher Power*.

"I hope there is, but when you look around at which war we will talk about today or who will die of cancer, it is hard to find a benign design, isn't it?" he replied.

He died on April 29, 2002, after suffering several heart attacks. I think he knows now if there is a *Higher Power*.

We all have memories of when we were young when we've looked up to an idol we've placed on a pedestal and wished to be like them, only to discover later they are all fallen stars who were searching for the meaning of life, and like us have been secretly asking, "Where did I come from, why am I here and where am I going when I die?"

Many well-known musicians and bands of the 1960s, such the Rolling Stones, the Beatles, Cliff Richard, the Shadows, Van Morrison and many other famous names all cite Lonnie Donegan, the king of *skiffle* and acknowledge his influence on them becoming involved in pop or rock music. Lonnie's *skiffle* music played a major part in drawing me along the same pathway as Tommy Hicks, the lad with the Cockney accent from Bermondsey, London, who changed his name to Tommy Steele. He became Britain's answer to Elvis. Tommy decided his future was not in pop music because it would be short-lived, and after making a few light-hearted movies he turned to drama and acted on stage.

Buddy Holly, Fats Domino, Jerry Lee Lewis, Little Richard and Elvis Presley are regarded as the legends of rock music. Many who came after them changed the style of 1950s rock music. These performers were named *leg-ends*.

I practised the guitar every free minute I had and tried to improve until I was playing as well as them. I acted out their moves on stage while I stood in front of my bedroom mirror.

Mum and Dad must have recognised I had finally found something I could stick to because they bought me my first guitar, which was a real financial sacrifice. Bert Weedon's book, *Play In A Day*, plus lessons from a man who knew the *three-chord trick* — E, A, and B7th, plus my daily practice, which resulted in the tips of my fingers being raw, enabled me to succeed. This effort reminded me of the song, *It's been a hard day's night*. Then I taught others such as George Jones who later had a very successful music and broadcasting career on Downtown Radio, BBC Radio Ulster, and U105. George and I formed our first skiffle group, which consisted of two or more guitar players, a washboard that improvised as percussion, a tea chest and a broom handle with a string of cord attached to it to improvise the sound of a bass. Along with *Jonsey* as he was known. We all had nicknames. I was known as

Dunner, and, of course, there was *Van the Man,* the Northern Irish rock legend. We stood on street corners where we loved strumming guitars while someone tapped the beat on the washboard and we sang the songs of Lonnie Donegan, *Putting On The Style, Rock Island Line, I'm Going To Rock My Soul In the Bosom Of Abraham,* and everyone's favourite, *It Takes A Worried Man To Sing A Worried Song.*

Bill playing in one of his street group's

Jonsey and I got our first taste of success when our *skiffle* group played in the Strand Cinema on Holywood Road at the Saturday morning matinee. Later that year we entered a talent contest at the old Empire Theatre in the centre of Belfast where we got into the final. We all agreed that the show was rigged; it must have been, because we lost.

The music back then was innocent fun, until the style changed. From across the Atlantic a new sound was born — *Rock n' Roll.* Our lives would never be the same again.

Chapter Three

"Rock Around the Clock"

(Song written by Max C. Freedman and James E. Myers)

"Music is spiritual," said Jimmy Hendrix, the rock legend who died of an overdose of drugs. Hendrix spoke openly about the spiritual aspect of music when he said, "Atmospheres are going to come through music because music is a spiritual thing of its own. You can hypnotise people with music, and when you get them at their weakest point you can preach into their subconscious whatever you want to say."[1]

When you've spent all of your teenage years up into your early twenties as a rock musician you won't disagree with the late Jimmy Hendrix. We discovered from experience how to use music to lift a crowd and excite their emotions, then change the mood and bring them down.

Music is used as a sales ploy, from selling sex to selling cars, even to getting a tooth filled. If you've ever waited in a dentist's surgery for your name to be called, calm soothing music is often playing in the background. That's to blot out the squeals of someone having a tooth drilled in the room next door; it's very thoughtful of them, isn't it?

Prior to my fourteenth birthday I formed a rock 'n' roll group, it was as if a child had been born and I looked after it as though it was one. It

---

1 Extract from Life magazine, October 3, 1969.

would be one of many that I would be part of on my musical journey in rock 'n' roll.

In the beginning, the bands I formed or played with, performed at talent contests and charity concerts. When we became semi-professional, we progressed into dance halls, night clubs and the Irish show-band scene. I frequented the Northern Ireland circuit — the Flamingo in Ballymena, the Belfast halls, the Plaza, Fiesta, and Romano's the Orpheus. Who from Belfast in the early 1960s, doesn't remember Betty Staffs? Climbing those stairs then jiving the night away to a live band in a hall so small you couldn't swing a cat in it. But it was exciting, to think you could hold a crowd of teeny-boppers in the palm of your hand as they screamed around the stage hoping for your attention. At the end of the night they hung around the back door of the hall wanting your autograph. But it was all a mirage soon to fade.

I was not aware at the time of the darkening shadows that would later overtake me and the slippery slope I was standing on. Had I known, I would have avoided the pitfalls.

It wasn't until I got into the rock music culture that I began drinking heavily and gambling seven card stud poker in the back of the minibus as we drove to and from the gigs.

Jonsey, Van, I, and others in the music business were semi-professional and hoping for the big breakthrough that would catapult us into the music limelight as full-time professionals. The Beatles were singing, *Money can't buy me love,* but we discovered you need money to pay the bills, so we all had a day job, then at night and weekends we were somewhere across the country, rocking the night away into the wee small hours of the morning.

There's a price to pay for burning the candle at both ends and pay day usually rewards you with health issues both physical and mental.

When I worked as a painter and decorator during the day and lived the life of a semi-professional singer at night and on weekends, the pressure began to build. On top of this, I was training in the Territorial Army (T.A.) Army Reserves, as it's known today. My mates and I signed up for two years to earn more money so we could purchase a motorcycle. We are stationed on the Antrim Road, Belfast with the Royal Engineers section. As the time of my commitment was coming to an end, I was losing interest in army life.

From left: Bill and his fellow soldier Ken – 1960

I never got into the drug scene as such; alcohol was what I turned to — a drug acceptable to many.

The usual set up for each gig was getting our gear out of the minibus and on to the stage, then making sure the instruments were in tune, before heading to the nearest bar to get tanked up. Seldom did I ever walk on to the stage sober. This created bouts of depression, something I had never experienced before in my life.

I remember one evening in particular playing to a packed house of teenyboppers in the Top Hat Ballroom, Lisburn. The girls were screaming and going wild at the front of the stage. In my drunken state, I looked out across the crowded floor and felt as if I was the loneliest person there. I had become part of the status quo, those who are rarely content with the way things are. I was desperately seeking to fill the emptiness inside me. As President Ronald Reagan once quipped, "The status quo … is Latin for the mess we're in."

Rock n' Roll I Gave You The Best Years Of My Life was written by Australian singer/song writer, the late Kevin Johnston. I wonder what his thoughts were as he looked back over his life before he died in 2019.

I find it so cheesy when a church leader or a youth pastor at a Christian music event or a Sunday church service thinks it's cool and hip to motivate the audience with, *Let's Rock n' Roll.*

Bill with his first car

In 1954, a disc jockey from Cleveland, America by the name of Alan Freed was searching for a name to best describe a new music sound pioneered by Buddy Holly, Ritchie Valens, and *The Big Bopper* (J.

P. Richardson) when they were killed in a plane crash on February 3, 1959, on their way to a gig. This incident became known as, *The Day The Music Died*, after Don McLean coined it in his 1971 song, *American Pie*. But the music didn't die. Chuck Berry, Elvis Presley, Jerry Lee Lewis and a host of others who made it big in the music business came along later and the music went global.

Alan Freed finally found a name he borrowed from a ghetto term that described premarital sex in the back seat of a car, the name was *rock and roll*. Many have since forgotten Alan Freed, but you can't go anywhere today without rock music blaring in your ears and the culture that it breeds, rebellion and low morality.

As the years progressed, rock music took on a more sinister side as a number of rock singers and songwriters dabbled in the occult and witchcraft and used backward masking in song lyrics to hide messages which it was believed could enter the subconscious mind.

In my gospel crusades and missions I had a night for youth where I preached themes such as, *Who is Messing With Your Head?* or *I Sold My Soul For Rock n' Roll*.

At these special youth rallies, I demonstrated backward masking and exposed the hidden dangers while lifting up the name of Jesus who said, *"The thief does not come except to steal, and to kill, and to destroy. I have come that they may have life, and that they may have it more abundantly"* John 10:10, NKJV. This resulted in many young people coming to Jesus and turning their lives around. Several brought their record collections to be burnt and destroyed.

One Halloween night we organised a bonfire at a special youth event in the town of Carrickfergus where we burnt a large collection of records, tapes and occult paraphernalia. Acts 19:19 KJV, records what the followers of Jesus did in the first century, *"Also, many of those who had practised magic brought their books together and burned them in the sight of all."* You can check out backward masking on Google and social media platforms.

During the 1980s, I was invited to give a talk and a presentation at a large youth camp in Gosford Forest Park, County Armagh. This was a week of various youth events organised by the Church of Ireland to reach both the churched and the non-churched youth. A panel of four questioned me to see if there was any truth and validity in what I was teaching. It consisted of a D.J. from a Belfast Radio Station, a nurse, a psychologist and a young man from the audience.

It went well and I survived the barrage of questions.

What the audience didn't see was what happened after the large tent was empty. I was approached by three young Christians who had brought a non-Christian lad of seventeen who had come to seek help. We moved into a smaller tent that was used for prayer and to talk. As he opened up, he told the tale of being a boy when his dad bought him his first heavy metal record album. He said this started his interest in the occult. His bedroom was filled with pictures of heavy metal regalia occult signs and symbols.

As he talked, his body language showed all the hallmarks of fear and self-doubt; he was sweating profusely, his eyes were staring and he rubbed his hands together vigorously. I asked if he was willing to receive Jesus Christ as his Saviour and confess Him Lord of his life, and denounce the devil and all his works. When I mentioned the blood Jesus shed on the Cross for the forgiveness of his sin, he fell to the ground and wriggled about in the grass like a serpent before he lay at my feet motionless — the young man was possessed by a demon.

But there, in that tent, Jesus set him free and gave him victory over what had been controlling him for years.

Bill standing outside one of his tent crusades

It is written in the Bible in Genesis 3:1–5, that the devil is seen entering the Garden of Eden as the subtle serpent who tempts Eve to disobey God. Adam quickly follows Eve with his disobedience, which results in sin entering the world and the death sentence being passed upon all humankind because of the sin of disregarding God's command — this is the bad news. But when we come to the last book in the Bible we read the good news, *"The dragon was cast out, that old serpent, called the devil, and satan, which deceives the whole world: he was cast out into the world, and his (fallen) angels were cast out with him. And I heard a loud voice saying in heaven, Now is come salvation, and strength, and the Kingdom of our God, and the power of his Christ: for the accuser of our brethren is cast down, which accused them before our God, day and night. And they overcame him by the blood of the Lamb, and the by the word of their testimony, and they loved not their lives unto death"* Revelation 12:9–11.

The devil doesn't have any feet to stand on, for he has been defeated by Christ who died for us on the Cross and rose to give us victory over the works of the devil, *"For this purpose the Son of God was manifested, that he might destroy the works of the devil"* 1 John 3:8, KJV.

You wouldn't let everyone who knocks on your door come in and make themselves at home, how much less that old serpent the devil. The bible says, *"Resist the devil and he will flee from you"* James 4:7, KJV.

Chapter Four

"Here Comes the Night"

(Song written by Bert Berns)

It was in early 1964, I was working as a painter/decorator on a building site, when I came home cold and tired. I hadn't planned anything for that particular evening so after dinner I just sat watching TV with some of my family. There was a knock at our front door.

"Who is that knocking at the door?" I asked my sister Agnes.

My mum went to see who it was.

"Does Billy Dunn live here?" asked a muffled voice.

Mum came back into the room.

"There's someone looking for Billy," she said.

I went into the hallway to see who it was and met this neatly dressed guy in a suit.

"I'm Billy Harrison," he said as he reached out his hand in a friendly gesture. "I'm starting an R&B Band and I need another lead vocalist who plays rhythm guitar. I've a lot of gigs lined up that will take us into the New Year and your name was passed on to me as someone who might be interested."

Indeed I was interested. Billy Harrison was not just at our front door but had come to ask me to join the birth of a new band. In case you don't know who Billy Harrison was, he was the founder of the band, *the Gamblers* who changed their name to *Them* and stormed onto the British music scene back in 1965 with, *Here Comes The Night,* which reached number 2, and *Baby Please Don't Go,* reached number 10. You will be interested to know what came about after that meeting with Billy Harrison; I shall return to that life-changing meeting later.

Television was a welcome distraction that offered escapism from the mundane and hum-drum of life in those days. All the families in our area huddled around their sets in the evenings, and if you were passing a house you could see the blue glow from the television shining around the edges of the curtains. It was often through watching the shows that I picked up and learnt great songs of the day.

Bill with Van Morrison

Michael Holiday was a popular British singer in the 1950s who had a tremendous voice. I used to watch him on Friday nights on the old black and white TV. He was clever and used a tape recorder to have a conversation with his own pre-recorded voice and then sang along with it. His timing was perfect and he looked so relaxed. But inside this man who entertained us on our TV screens, we couldn't see that he was disturbed.

There's a song he made popular at the time, *Some day I'm gonna write, the story of my life. I'll tell about the night we met and how my heart can't forget, the way you smiled at me.* Some day? Michael Holiday never got round to writing the story of his life.

He suffered stage fright and a deep sense of dissatisfaction with himself which became so unbearable that he committed suicide.

Although television was such a welcome distraction there were the advertisements ...

Have you ever wondered why we are bombarded with advertisements on TV and in magazines that promise life-changing formulas only for us to discover later on that the promises fall far short of our expectations? They are like bait to fish; they are trying to find out what will hook us. If they can find out what hooks us then they know they will have a client and you and I know what that means — our hard-earned money will go from our pocket into theirs.

Going back to that knock at the door I mentioned earlier. Billy Harrison was the brains and founder of the famous R & B band *Them*.

When they appeared on Top of the Pops, the vocalist was my buddy Van Morrison, who left the band in 1967.

There can never be peaceful agreement or differences resolved when two strong personalities clash head-to-head — someone, or something has to give.

The story was taken up by a Belfast tabloid, and if I remember correctly it was *City Beat,* who told the story about the break-up of the band. It was after that, that Van left to pursue a successful career in America, which brought him the popularity and success he revels in today.

As the group's lead vocalist I was on my way at last to fame and fortune, so it seemed. I was soon to discover, like many others, how disillusioned I was. As the song says, *Here comes the night.*

Chapter Five

"You Light up my Senses ..."

(Song written by John Denver)

John Denver wrote one of his most beautiful songs for his wife, Ann Martell after their first separation and the near break-up of their marriage in 1974. The title is *Annie's Song*.

The lyrics, *You Light Up My Senses* were an expression of his exuberant feelings of joy. He said he was reflecting on all the joy he found in his marriage and his relief that he and Ann were back together.

Unfortunately, their marriage did not have a happily-ever-after ending and they divorced in 1982, because of the demands of his career.

Watch the movie and see for yourself. There is only one that can light up our senses without something or someone switching off the lights — that One is Jesus. John 8:18 says, "I am the light of the world: he who follows Me shall not walk in darkness, but shall have the light of life."

It was just past midnight on the May 19, 1965; I was sitting at home alone when I heard a voice in my head. I wasn't on *wacky-backy* smoking pot, neither was I losing it mentally. I was fully aware of what was going on in my life. This wasn't the first time I had heard this voice.

Several times over the years the voice had called me, only at this point in time it was coming more often and was much stronger. Earlier in the week my father had been rushed to the Royal Victoria Hospital in Belfast with a heart attack. As the week dragged on, Dad suffered several strokes.

Each night after work I drove across the city on a motorbike, picked up my girlfriend Iris, then drive to the hospital where we sat at Dad's bedside with Mum, hoping he would get well and be back home. But on May 18, 1965 at 10 p.m. he died leaving all the family heartbroken and with a deep chasm to fill in our lives.

Family are one of the most important values we have in life. If you died tonight your employer would advertise to fill your job role by the end of the month, but your loved ones, family and friends, would miss you forever. So don't get so busy making a living that you forget to make a life.

During the day at work, the voice in my head didn't bother me as much; it was when I got home after visiting in the hospital and dropping off Iris, when I was alone with my thoughts, that the voice in my head began talking, *What would you do Billy, if you were in the same situation as your dad, lying in a hospital bed about to die?*

I knew I didn't need a preacher, a pastor or a priest to tell me that if I was to die in the spiritual state I was living, I would go straight to hell. The voice was the voice of God. Some refer to it as their conscience speaking to them. It is God who gives us a conscience for us to decide between what is right and wrong and bring us to a decision about how we should live our lives —either our way or His way.

Often it was the same question He would ask me, *Billy, what would you gain if you had the whole world at your feet but lost your soul?*

This triggered something in my mind that I'd heard a year earlier while painting a school and working alongside another painter, a Christian named Eric McCullough. He explained a verse of scripture from Matthew 16:26, the words of Jesus, "What is a man profited if he gains the whole world, and loses his own soul? Or what will a man give in exchange for his soul."

The words were similar to the voice I was hearing in my head.

What impressed me most about Eric was he didn't talk about religion; he talked about Jesus, and was excited about what he was talking about. At first I thought he was on something, or smoking something, and I wanted what he had.

Back then I had the same idea as many who think the Christian life is boring and a drag — wear a black suit, a white shirt, black tie, part your hair in the middle with Brylcreem, carry a big black book — a Bible, and by all means don't smile in case God sees you enjoying yourself. Eric blew this philosophy out of the water. I witnessed his life, he *walked the talk*. I saw Jesus in him.

I believe God brings people into our lives or across the pathway that we are walking like a sign-post to point us in the right direction. On May 18, 1965, I arrived home from the hospital at about 10:30 p.m., made a cup of tea, lit a cigarette and sat down to watch TV. Back in the 1960s it was black and white TV and only two channels on a small 14-inch screen. I remember well that television seemed extra boring that night as I switched the channels back and forth from BBC1 to BBC2. Bored by what was on, I turned off the TV and reached into my record collection of favourite rock artists, Elvis Presley, Roy Orbison, Jerry Lee Lewis, and the Everly Brothers. As the voice of God again began to put thoughts into my mind, I picked out an album that had four gospel songs by Elvis and put it on the turntable in the hope the voice in my head would be drowned out by the music. I listened to the first song as I puffed on a cigarette, then lit another. It was the third song that spoke to me. At 12:20 a.m. on May 19, 1965, a new day had begun as Elvis sang:

Well I'm tired and I'm weary, but I must go along,
Till the Lord comes and calls, calls me away,
Well the morning is bright,
And the lamb is the light,
And the night is as black as the sea.
There will be peace in the valley for me ...

At that moment I fell to my knees and prayed to God to forgive me as I asked Jesus to come into my life and give me His peace. In the words of a gospel song written by Bill and Gloria Gather I can truthfully say, "Something happened and now I know, He touched me and He made me whole."

Immediately, all the negative thoughts that had built up over years of living life my way, the fear, the heavy weight of guilt that had weighed me down, lifted off my shoulders. I finally found what I had been searching for all my life that morning when Jesus came into my life and filled up my senses.

Whatever you walk away from, is what you have control over, whatever you don't walk away from controls you.

In 1938, when Albert Brumley published his classic gospel song, *Turn Your Radio On,* he exhorted his listeners on radio to "turn the lights down low and listen to the master's radio." If they would but "listen to the music in the air" then they, too, could "get in touch with God."

If you call upon God for forgiveness and peace when He comes to check you over you will discover He won't measure the size of your brain because He's too big to fit inside your head. He will check the size of your heart; how much you believe He is able and willing to do for you.

Something else happened in those early hours of that morning. I have already mentioned that as a child I was born with a health problem, chronic bronchitis.

Many times I had difficulty breathing and Mum often took me to our local GP where I was prescribed *malt*. I must have eaten enough malt over the years to sink a battleship. But on May 19, 1965, at 12:20 a.m. without any medical help or a doctor's prescription Jesus Christ came into my life and healed me and I've had no problem with my lungs or my breathing ever since.

The alcohol went out of the window, cigarettes went out of the window, playing cards went out of the window and fear and anxiety went out of the window also. There were a lot of broken windows in 16 Greenville Street on that early morning when Jesus walked in and set this captive free.

"I have had many problems in my life of which most didn't happen," said Winston Churchill. We can all relate to this — crossing bridges before we get to them — fear of things that never materialise. Like many today fear was the monkey that often sat on my shoulder until Jesus came and knocked it off.

Being uncertain about what might be around the next corner, unsure of where the journey in life is leading is one of the root causes of fear and poor mental health.

I read the story about the famous scientist Albert Einstein, who was leaving on a train journey to an out-of-town engagement. The conductor stopped to punch his train ticket. The great scientist, preoccupied with his work, rummaged through his coat pockets and briefcase for his ticket. Much to his embarrassment — it wasn't there.

"We all know who you are, Dr Einstein. I'm sure you bought a ticket. Don't worry about it," said the conductor graciously.

"Everything is okay," said the conductor as he walked down the aisle punching other tickets. Before he moved to the next carriage he looked back and saw Dr Einstein on his hands and knees looking under his seat trying to find his ticket. He rushed back. "Dr Einstein, please don't worry about it," he said. "I know who you are," he added.

The great Einstein looked up. "I, too, know who I am. What I don't know is where I'm going," he replied.

This amazing God who turned life's tests into a triumphant testimony and my messed-up life into a meaningful message stands waiting to do the same for all, the moment they hand their lives over to Him.

Since Jesus Christ died and rose from the dead we can have as much of God as we want. This infinite God can give all of Himself to each and every one who by faith have received Christ as their Saviour and Lord. He does not distribute Himself that each might only have a part, but to each one He gives all of Himself as fully as if there are no others. Jesus said, *"Come to Me, all you who labour and are heavy laden, and I will give you rest. Take My yoke upon you and learn from Me, for I am gentle and lowly in heart, and you will find rest for your souls"* Matthew 11:28, NKJV.

We all have our emotional basements and attics where we hide our clutter — regrets we have over past mistakes, grudges we hold on to, hurts we hide under clouds of anger, and fear of the unexpected. While all this emotional clutter might be eating us up inside or weighing us down the medical and psychological faculty who reach out a hand to help us, know they are far from winning the battle against mental illness. I have found the answer — *"You wilt keep him in perfect peace, whose mind is stayed on You, because he trusts in You. Trust in the Lord forever"* Isaiah 26:3, NKJV.

It was not only the change of losing the desire for alcohol, gambling, smoking, and other stuff that had messed up my life that convinced me Jesus Christ rose from the dead and was now living in my life, but also the moment I got saved, I began to read the Bible, I literally devoured it. I carried a small Bible to work in the top pocket of my overalls where I previously kept my cigarettes. When the other guys stopped for a smoke I stopped for a Bible reading.

Every night when I retired to bed I sat up reading and studying this life-transforming book until two or three in the morning, knowing I had work the next day.

Reading was never one of my great interests or favourite pastimes. I'm a practical person, a hands-on guy. As I wrote earlier, the only thing I ever liked about school was the half past three bell. When it rang, I was free to do what I loved most — pick up my guitar and sing. But the Bible had replaced the music. I had a desire similar to the prophet Jeremiah who said, *"Your words were found, and I ate them. And Your word was to me the joy and rejoicing of my heart."* Jeremiah *15:16. I couldn't get enough of this life changing word of the living God. 'The word of God, which Paul says, "effectively works in you who believes"* 1 Thessalonians 2:13, NKJV.

Chapter Six

"When I Fall in Love ..."

(Song written by Victor Young and Edward Heyman)

The song *When I Fall In Love* has become a standard with artists such as Nat King Cole, Rick Astley, Michael Bublé and many others who have recorded it; the first hit version by Doris Day was released in July 1952. *When I fall in love, it will be forever, or I'll never fall in love. In a restless world like this is, Love is ended before it's begun ...* the truth about Doris Day's four tumultuous marriages is heart-breaking. She discovered that falling in love is not forever.

In the book *The Four Loves* by C. S. Lewis he makes a powerful observation about love being vulnerable. He says that there is *no safe investment* when a person risks loving. He suggests that loving anything will lead to your heart being wrung and possibly broken.

It was Monday September 26, 2016, and my heart was wrung and broken when Iris, the love of my life went to heaven after fifty-six years of a marriage that had been filled with love, happiness and fulfilment. *"He who finds a wife finds a good thing, and obtains favour from the Lord"* Proverbs 18:22, NKJV.

How did we start a relationship that lasted so long? If I wasn't out singing with the band, I was out with my mates on a Saturday night at one of the many dance halls in the city, Betty Staffs, The Fiesta, Romano's, The Orpheus and other venues in the country.

It was a Saturday night — July 1964. Me and the lads went to the Plaza in Chichester Street, Belfast. The usual procedure was to buy a ticket at the door then ask for a pass out before we headed for the nearest bar. The craic in the bar was so good that we lost all sense of time and had to rush back. The six of us broke into pairs and quickly scoured the packed dance floor, which was filled with gyrating bodies twisting and shaking to the beat of the loud music. We were looking for a couple of pretty girls who were looking for two handsome, hunky guys. I had been paired off with a childhood friend called Billy Phillips. "There's two out there," he shouted above the noise of the music.

We pushed our way through the crowd who were all doing *the Twist* which was the latest craze at the time. We joined in without being invited. When the music stopped, I introduced myself.

"I'm Billy, what's your name?"

"Iris," she replied.

The band played a few more upbeat songs as we jived and did the twist and enjoyed ourselves. When it was over, as we walked off the floor my mate asked where they lived. "Off the top the Old Park Road," they said in harmony. We asked to escort them home.

We caught a bus that took us to the bus stop near to the Park Cinema. "This is where we get off," said Iris.

The four of us arranged to meet the following Wednesday night. After that night my mate Billy and Iris's friend called it off. But Iris and I agreed that we would meet outside the Plaza the next Saturday night.

I arrived early all dressed up and with my aftershave on, but Iris didn't turn up.

"Ah well," I said to myself as I hid my disappointment. "There's plenty more fish in the sea." I went in for a coffee then caught a bus home.

I thought it was over between Iris and me and that I would never see her again, but what a surprise when she turned up at my door with her friend later that week. During our conversation on the Saturday night when we met, I said I lived at Greenville Street in Bloomfield. How she found out exactly where I lived was interesting. She stopped at the first house she came to in the street and asked a complete stranger where Billy Dunn lived.

The three of us were talking when my sister Agnes and my brother-in-law Jackie drove up in the car.

"I recognise you two girls," said my sister. "You were standing around the corner off May Street last Saturday night."

"No, it wasn't us," replied Iris' friend. Both looked guilty.

"Oh yes, it was," said my sister. "We were sitting in a bar across the road watching you both juking back and forth around the corner looking down Chichester Street. We wondered what you were up to."

No one knows who could be watching us.

The Bible says, *"You are the God who sees me"* Genesis 16:13, NKJV. Little did they know they were being watched. When my sister and her husband went into the house Iris explained what had happened. Every Saturday night she and her friend went to a dance. When we had arranged to meet she thought my pal and her friend would also be there, but later she was told that they had decided they weren't interested in each other. So, not wanting to leave her friend alone on a Saturday night and yet wanting to meet me, she decided to put her friend first and meet me at another time and explain then. This she did that night when they both travelled from the Old Park in North Belfast to Bloomfield in the east of the city. Here was a girl who put her friend before herself; someone who was beautiful on the outside while beautiful on the inside, which greatly impressed me. From that moment on we began to date and became a couple.

Iris and I were not Christians when we met, but within a few years we discovered the amazing plan God had for our lives and the wonderful relationship He had brought us together to enjoy them.

We had the same interests — music, films, and days out in the city and further afield on my motorbike. Certainly we had our moments when we didn't see eye to eye and agree on everything. The Bible says, *"As iron sharpens iron, so a man sharpens the countenance of his friend"* Proverbs 27:17, NKJV.

Iris most definitely sharpened me on some issues while knocking off some of my rough edges.

On any given Sunday if she found me playing poker she let me know how she felt. At first she was excited about me playing in the band. She was being dated by a rock singer and she told her sisters and her friends, but as time moved on and I was out more often with the band the excitement began to wear off. I realised this when she started dropping hints that I should spend more time with her and less time travelling in the old Bedford mini bus to gigs.

Iris' father, Tommy Duff was a Christian who desired to see his three daughters Eleanor, Iris and Marion saved and walking in the ways of the Lord, but his constant preaching and strict religious views put them off. So when I accepted the faith Iris was not one bit pleased. It came to boiling point and we had to decide the direction our relationship was going in. I prayed a lot about it and came up with the idea of a bargaining chip. If she came to a Saturday night gospel meeting in the

Coalmen's Mission, on the same night I would treat her to a first-class meal at whatever restaurant she chose.

We had an excellent meal, but what was even better — that night at the Coalmen's Mission, the Spirit of God spoke to her and Iris became a Christian. And what a tremendous *help-meet* she became, especially when we entered the ministry and began pastoring the church. Her computer skills were a great help, and her smile and personality were infectious. She drew people she had met earlier in the week while out shopping and invited them to the Sunday meetings to hear the best gospel singer and preacher in town. Even though Iris was tone deaf and hit every right note in the wrong place she always encouraged me; she had more confidence in me than I had in myself.

Genesis chapter two is the story of the first two genders God created — they were, of course, male and female — Adam and Eve who were deeply in love. When you read chapter two it is interesting to see that although God put Adam into a beautiful environment called the Garden of Eden and gave him everything he wanted for his enjoyment, verse eighteen of chapter two reveals that Adam was incomplete without a woman. And the Lord God said, "It is not good that man should be alone; I will make him a help-meet comparable to himself." And Iris was a tremendous *help-meet* — a helper in every sense of the word.

Whenever we were together I often said to Iris, "I like you." Until one beautiful summer evening I fell in love and I looked into her beautiful eyes. "I love you; I want to spend the rest of my life with you," I said.

That night I went to bed singing. *A well I bless my soul. What's wrong with me? I'm itching like a man on a fuzzy tree. My friends say I'm actin' wild as a bug. I'm in love. I'm all shook up.*

We'd met in July 1964, and married in the spring of 1966, and went to the Isle of Bute in Scotland for our honeymoon. God called Iris home to heaven on the September 26, 2016. How does one handle a broken heart?

> *Life is an ocean and love is a boat*
> *In troubled water that keeps us afloat*
> *When we started the voyage, there was just you and me*
> *Now gathered around us, we have our own crew.*
> (*The Voyage* by Christy Moore, Irish Folk Singer)

One of many heart-breaking images that sticks in the mind is from the Duke of Edinburgh's funeral in 2021. It is a picture of Queen Elizabeth.

Because of pandemic restrictions, the Queen spent the service sitting on her own — a solitary figure, surrounded by rows and rows of empty pews, as she bid farewell to her husband of seventy-three years — a broken-hearted lady.

A broken heart is the one thing we all suffer from. It touches the hardest among us, the rich and the poor and it cuts through all skin colours.

Recently, while I was driving in the country, a song came on the radio that I'd forgotten about, *The Living Years* by Mike and the Mechanics.

Every generation blames the one before, and all of their frustrations come beating at the door. I know that I'm a prisoner to all my father held so dear, I know that I'm a hostage to all his hopes and fears. I just wish I could have told him, in the living years.

This song is about living with regrets. It is written from the perspective of a son who has never had a good relationship with his father because of the vast difference in their generations. His father's generation was about hard work and responsibility while his generation was about having fun. After his father dies, he discovers that he and his dad had a much stronger bond than he ever realised, and he regrets not being more demonstrative while his dad was alive.

As I cruised and listened to the song I was moved to tears by the words, *I wasn't there that morning when my father passed away. I didn't get to tell him all the things I had to say. I think I caught his spirit later that same year, I'm sure I heard his echo in my baby's new born tears. I wish I could have told him, in the living years ...*

At such times when memories come flooding in about the living years of missed opportunities to express love to bygone family and friends I whisper a prayer and ask the Lord for grace to help me through. In the Bible book of Hebrews, chapter four, verse sixteen it says, *"We may obtain mercy and find grace to help in time of need."* The good news is, *"He heals the broken hearted and binds up their wounds"* Psalm 147:3, KJV.

Don't hold back from telling those near and dear to you, family and friends, I love you. Fill your home every day with these words and you will be amazed how peace will flood your heart.

A broken heart is the one thing we never get over, but we can get through it. God's word says: *"The Lord is close to the broken hearted"* Psalm 34:18, NIV.

While a miracle is instantaneous, healing is a process — it takes time. So, as the binding of a wound over a period of time brings healing, the Lord binds our broken heart with grace to help us. With time the healing process will be at that moment when Jesus Christ returns as King of kings and Lord of lords as he wipes away all tears from our eyes, and makes all things new.[2]

With regard to the second coming of Jesus Christ the Bible says, *"The Lord Himself shall descend from heaven with a shout, with the voice of an*

---

2 Revelation 21:4-5.

archangel, and with the trumpet of God. And the dead in Christ will rise *first. Then we who are alive and remain shall be caught up with them in* *the clouds to meet the Lord in the air. And thus we shall always be with* *the Lord. Therefore comfort one another with these words"* 1 Thessalonians 4:16-18, NKJV.

Don't be afraid to fall in love, and never draw back from giving love to someone even though your heart may one day be broken. The experience of giving love and receiving it far outweighs the hurt.

I'm looking forward to that day when I will see Iris again, and many of my family members and loved ones in their glorified body in the *Father's house.* This is what Jesus promises all His followers, *"Let not* *your heart be troubled: ye believe in God, believe also in me. In my Father's* *house are many mansions: if it were not so, I would have told you. I go* *to prepare a place for you. And if I go and prepare a place for you, I will* *come again, and receive you unto myself; that where I am, there ye may* *be also"* John 14:1-3, KJV.

In her book, *Heaven: My Father's House[3],* Anne Graham Lotz writes about the time she bought a ticket for a tour of Buckingham Palace in London. She passed through one spectacular room after another, gazing at the hand-painted ceilings, magnificent, museum-quality tapestries, masterpieces of art, priceless porcelains, gilded furniture, crystal chandeliers, and other treasures too numerous and awesome to describe. But nowhere did she see a child's toy, or a family photograph, or an open magazine, or a jacket casually thrown over a chair, or a table set for two, or even a coffee cup sitting on a side table. "As I expected," she wrote, "Buckingham Palace is a magnificent showplace, but it's hard to think of it as a *home.*"

"While my *Father's House* is the most beautiful place ever imagined, it's not a museum or a mere showplace — it is definitely home. It's

3 Anne Graham Lotz. Heaven *My Father's House,* Nashville. W Publishing Group, 2014 93.

the home of the Lord God Almighty and the Lamb." In the book of Revelation John says, *"I did not see a temple in the city, because the Lord God Almighty and the Lamb are its temple"* Revelation 21:22, NIV.

Bill and Iris with family 1994

Knowing where you are going takes the uncertainty out of getting there.

The glittering scenes of heaven recorded in the book of Revelation will far exceed anything in Buckingham Palace, yet it will be the heavenly home of every born-again believer in Christ.

Our resurrected and glorified bodies will be perfectly equipped to enjoy all the features of our home in the new heaven and new earth. Our friends and loved ones in Christ will meet us in the New Jerusalem. Our tears will be gone forever, and our years will have no end."

One is not surprised to read that the last recorded prayer in the Bible prayed by John is, *"Even so come Lord Jesus"* Revelation 22:20, KJV.

Chapter Seven

"It Ain't Necessarily So ..."

(Song written by Ira Gershwin)

In 2013, British actor, David Suchet was filming the final TV episodes as Agatha Christie's beloved Belgian detective Hercule Poirot and also starring in a stage play when he took on the biggest role of his life. Between those projects he recorded an audio version of the entire Bible, from Genesis to Revelation, 752,702 words, which took over two hundred hours. Suchet, who became a believer in Jesus Christ after reading the book of Romans in a Bible he found in a hotel room, took on this project and said, "It was the fulfilment of a twenty-seven-year-long ambition. I felt totally driven. I did so much research on every part of it that I couldn't wait to get going." Then he donated his wages.

Not everyone shares the same view as a Bible-believing Christian. The Bible has come under attack more than any other book.

They have tried to ban it, burn it, bury it, and blaspheme it, yet it remains the world's best seller. I find it amusing when someone shows their ignorance by saying that the Bible is a book of fairy tales; that no intelligent person could believe. Then at Christmas time they tell their child the fairy tale that there's a man with a big white beard, wearing a red suit, and he'll be coming down the chimney on Christmas night with presents.

If the Bible is a book of fairy tales they have nothing to fear, a fairy tale can't do them any harm. But deep down inside there is the fear many have of opening a Bible and being exposed to its truth — *you need to change your sinful lifestyle.* The façade and their ego is stripped away.

The Bible was written over a period of sixteen hundred years by many different authors. It has a red strand running throughout from Genesis to Revelation with this theme, *"Without the shedding of blood there is no remission for sin."* And that blood is, *"The blood of Jesus Christ His Son cleanses us from all sin"* 1 John 1:7, NKJV.

The words to *It Ain't Necessarily So,* were written by Ira Gershwin and the music was composed by George Gershwin for their 1935 opera Porgy and Bess. It's a song that expresses doubt about stories in the Bible and is seen as a subtle attack on the Word of God. It hit the pop charts in the early 1960s.

It ain't necessarily so, It ain't necessarily so, the things you are liable to read in the Bible, it ain't necessarily so.

What is it that causes people to dislike the Bible so much? Is it because they think that they are agents of free will and they don't like being told how they should live their lives, or is it because it disturbs their conscience? Perhaps they think if they don't read the Bible and just keep their heads buried in the sand like the proverbial ostrich, on judgment day they can plead ignorance is bliss?

It's the book that has the answer to many of life's problems. It's the only book that shows us the way we can find peace with God.

An evangelistic organisation sent a team to Stavropol, Russia, in 1994, to hand out Bibles that had been locked away when Stalin was sending believers in Jesus Christ to the gulags. Among those who showed up was a young agnostic student just wanting to earn a day's wages. But he soon slipped away.

An older team member went looking for him and found him sitting in a corner weeping. Out of the hundreds of Bibles, he had picked up one that bore the handwritten signature of his grandmother. Persecuted for her faith, she had prayed often for her family, her city and this young man. God used that grandmother's Bible to convict him of his need for Jesus that day. This is what so many fear regarding the Bible. Such is the power of God's Word.

If today's generation opened a Bible as often as they open their mobile phones their lives would be transformed and communities would change for the better.

The book of Habakkuk 2:12 gives this promise, *"The earth shall be filled with the knowledge of the glory of the Lord, as the waters cover the sea."*

God's Word needs to be read daily, read prayerfully, read thoughtfully and read believingly because it has the power to change lives today.

Chapter Eight

"A Wonderful World ..."

(Song written by Bob Thiele aka George Douglas)

God must have a sense of humour. Three months after I was converted or born-again depending on how you explain it, I received the call of God to enter the Church ministry. Me, of all people, who never liked school — God was calling me to Bible college. It was a call that Iris and I thought seriously about.

Iris and I were married in 1966, Paul was born on Boxing Day 1967 and bills were piling up. How could we raise the fees for college? Something else stood in the way. I believed Jesus could return to earth for His people at any moment, in the blink of an eye. And if that happened I wouldn't want to be sitting in some stuffy old Bible college studying books, time was too short. Besides all this, the college I was thinking about was in England which meant I would have to leave a young wife and child that I loved and set sail across to mainland Britain. Did I go?

There's a wealth of wisdom in the saying, *To fail to prepare is to prepare to fail?* Yes, I did go. God doesn't want us to leave our brains outside on the church porch every time we enter a worship service, neither does He want us to sit through a church service critically analysing all that's going on. There is the need to be evenly balanced. The Bible says, *"Study to show yourself approved to God"* 2 Timothy 2:15. It also says in 2 Corinthians 5:7, *"We walk by faith, not by sight."*

Bill and Iris on their wedding day, 1966.

Since entering the 21st Century we have seen big changes take place on a world-wide scale both good and bad, but we need to block out the negative media in its attempts to make us believe that everything we read in the newspaper or watch on TV is the truth, especially many of the lies and conspiracy theories on social media. The atheistic psychologist, the agnostic psychiatrist and others from such camps who have hatched their conspiracy theories that God is extinct are not having it all their own way. It appears that twenty-first-century science agrees with ancient scripture that God cannot be analysed in a laboratory, worked out in a test-tube experiment, and it cannot be proven philosophically that He is not personally involved in creation.

Reliable scientists are now affirming how ingenious God is and how His principles hold up under the piercing light of scientific scrutiny. In his book, *How God Changes Your Brain: Breakthrough Findings From a Leading Neuroscientist.*[4] neuroscientist Andrew Newberg MD, who studies the relationship between spiritual phenomena and the brain, has demonstrated that we were designed physically and mentally to interact with God through prayer and scripture. It's a known fact that

---

4 New York Ballantine Books 2010.

there are centres in the human brain, which respond positively to prayer, reading and meditating on God's word, group worship, hymn singing, and empathy for other people. Dr Newberg believes that practising a personal religious faith is the most powerful way to maintain a healthy brain. The brain's frontal lobe is used to focus attention for rational thinking and decision making.

It responds to prayer and meditation by helping reduce stress, strengthen our immune system, enhance memory, and increase our capacity for compassion. It helps us ward off age-related brain deterioration and live longer. Newberg's research indicates that praying for at least twelve minutes a day slows age-related brain decline. Prayer and reading scripture also deactivates areas of the brain associated with anger, guilt, anxiety, depression, fear, resentment, and pessimism.

People talk about heaven being so far away, but to those who pray it is within speaking distance. Gone are the days when weak-kneed theologians bowed to the god of science.

University or Bible college may not be for everyone, but it was for me. And if it's not for you don't worry, I recently read a list of names of famous people who never graduated.

Andrew Carnegie, US industrialist and philanthropist
Charles Chaplin, British actor and film director
Noel Coward, British actor, playwright, and composer
Charles Dickens, British novelist
Thomas Edison, US inventor
Maxim Gorky, Russian writer
Claude Monet, French painter
Sean O'Casey, Irish playwright
Henry M Stanley, British explorer
Mark Twain, writer.

It wasn't long after arriving at Elim Bible College in England when my eyes were opened and I saw that Bible College was an unreal world that could give a false sense of security. Why? Because everyone had been placed in a bubble where each one was walking close to God, and the devil was far away, nearly as if — you had arrived in heaven. Such a thought was far from the truth.

I was to reside in a dorm with five other guys from different parts of the world, all with different personalities. My time in the college was an education in how to live in peace with all men; far more beneficial that the theological education that was being offered.

Bible College students and teachers.

It was 1970, and the first term ran from September to Christmas. It was the first of several occasions that I would be away from Iris and young son Paul. But we believed it was the will of God to help prepare us for the ministry He was calling us to.

At the end of the first term, Rev. Wynn Lewis, a fiery wee Welshman, who lectured on the subject of *Youth Ministries* gave us a task over the Christmas and New Year period. We were to go to the largest church in our city or town and interview the minister and youth leader about the steps that they were taking to reach the youth in their area.

I contacted the legendary, late Rev. Sam Workman, minister of the Congregational Church at Whiteabbey, who was seeing many conversions in his Sunday services and numerical growth. During my meeting with him, he gave me my bus fare home.

On the bus home I was stirred by the thought of Belfast, the city I grew up in, and how it had become a divided city — Catholic and Protestant. The 1970s saw a lot of bombing and shooting which caused devastation. An idea came to me that I should contact one of the Catholic chapels to interview the priest in charge. This was accepted by the Roman Catholic Church and convent at the top of Ravenhill Road. I was greeted warmly by a sprightly thirty-five-year-old — imagine remembering his age and not his name — a sure sign I am getting older.

We chatted for a brief while and I was introduced to the youth leader who showed me around, and explained the set-up for youth which was impressive.

After the tour I was brought back to the priest's office where I discovered a new arrival was seated —the priest of Religious Studies.

With a notepad and pen, I began to ask questions relating to the work and programmes the church offered to youth in Belfast. Every question I asked, either to the priest or to the youth leader, this guy interjected.

Near the end of the meeting, I turned to the youth leader and asked what he thought about why the youth of our city was so bent on mayhem and destruction. I had no sooner finished speaking when this guy, the head of Religious Studies got all shook up with the question. 'I'll tell you why, our people don't have anything and they are making sure the other side will be the same,' he said in an angry voice.

'I'm not talking to you, I'm asking this young man the question,' I replied. As if he was a little boy who had been chastised for speaking out of turn, he kept his mouth closed for the rest of the evening.

He might have been the head of Religious Studies, but he needed some serious spiritual heart surgery as we all do, from the One who said, *Love your enemies, do good to those who hate you, bless those who curse you, and pray for those who spitefully use you.* Luke 6:27–28, NKJV.

There is a danger of over emphasising a university education or a college degree to the detriment of a personal heart experience with God. We don't need half the alphabet after our names, a high-ranking position or a celebrity status to bring about change for the better of the planet we live on, or to influence others. We don't say, *I love you with my head,* we usually say, *I love you with all my heart.* One has to strike the right balance when living the Christian life before the world. Jesus said, *"God is Spirit: and they who worship Him must worship Him in Spirit and in truth"* John 4:24.

You can go to any university in the world and study for a degree in almost any available subject from A to Z — archaeology to zoology and earn a BA, an MA, a PhD, but there is no university in the world that offers a PMA degree (A Positive Mental Attitude) that really works, this only comes about through a personal relationship with God by faith in Jesus Christ, a positive mental attitude — outlook on life that gives inner peace in this present world and eternal life in the world to come.

Bill in preaching mode

While pastoring a church in the north-east of England, I was invited to a minister's fraternal, a meeting of vicars, ministers and pastors from churches in the community who drink a lot of tea and coffee and often tried to impress one another with what their church was doing for the community and what they had accomplished so far in life.

That Friday morning the local vicar from the CE (Church of England) had recently received a PhD and was waxing eloquently.

We applauded him on his achievement and that opened up the conversation and everyone began to brag about their university degrees over tea and biscuits. One chap with a polite English accent drew everyone's attention when he turned to me.

"Pastor Dunn, what degree have you studied towards since coming into church ministry?" he asked.

All eyes were on me because they saw that he was talking down to me and they waited to see how I would respond. I replied with an answer that confused him. "I have received three B A's, the first when I was born and before I came to have faith in Jesus Christ; I was a *bad article*. The second one I received was when I was *born again* in 1965 when I received Jesus Christ as my Saviour. The third I earnt through study when I received a Bachelor of Arts Degree from college. Do you know anything about the first two, being a bad article and then being born again?" I replied and his eyes widened, then he became flustered and his face went red.

'The smallest package I have ever seen is a man all wrapped up in himself," said the great evangelist, the late Dr Billy Graham.

Jesus said, *"If ye have faith as a grain of mustard seed, ye shall say unto this mountain, remove hence to yonder place; and it shall remove; and nothing shall be impossible unto you"* Mathew 17:20, KJV.

In my personal experience, and in the lives of many to whom I ministered the Word of God — the gospel of His grace, I have seen souls saved, lives changed, mountains of fear melt, marriages restored, financial and business projects prosper, sickness healed and many other miracles. In May 2016, I was invited to sing at the Whitby Gospel Music Convention. On the last night of the event I was performing my set of songs and the final song I ended with was from my CD, *Rise And Be Healed.* As I sang the chorus line for the second time, *Rise and be healed in the name of Jesus, let faith arise in your soul. Rise and be healed in the name of Jesus, He will cleanse you and make you whole,* a lady in a wheelchair stood on her feet, raised her arms and fixed her eyes towards heaven.

She then turned around and to the amazement of many pushed her wheelchair out of the auditorium. Jesus said, *"With men this is impossible; but with God all things are possible"* Matthew 19:26, KJV.

A wonderful world indeed and yet, how much more is the world of the kingdom of heaven.

Chapter Nine

"I'm all Shook Up ..."

(Song written by Otis Blackwell)

Over the years I've been hounded by moguls of music magazines, tabloid newspapers, and even one sleazy character who was gathering material he said was for a book he hoped to write which had the title, *The Secret Life of Van Morrison.* He was merely after juicy gossip to make easy money at someone else's expense. "I'm not an animal, I don't carry a tale," I replied.

Everyone is entitled to a private life away from the glare of the world. For anyone to carry a tale that someone has shared with them about their private life is a low attempt at climbing to the top of the heap to make themselves popular with the crowd. Perhaps you understand the reason why celebrities and other public figures don't like giving interviews.

It was 1979 when I released my first album of gospel songs. In those days they were LP's, CD's were a thing of the future and live streaming was light years away. I wanted to make a statement so I named the album, *Thank God I am Free.*

The Daily Mirror got wind of it and made it a front-page item with the eye-catching headline, *The Singing Swinging Vicar* and then went on to talk about how I had turned my back on being a pop star for the pulpit scene.

BBC Radio Ulster saw it as an interesting item for their afternoon music and chat show hosted by Gloria Hunniford OBE and invited me to be interviewed by her.

When I arrived at this highly respected old building, BBC Broadcasting House in Ormeau Avenue in the centre of Belfast, I was rushed into the studio where she was wearing a large set of headphones they call cans, leaning forward in her chair and talking into a microphone. When she finished speaking she flicked on some music, switched off her mike, turned to me, smiled and shook my hand. She explained what was planned for the interview. She intended to play a track from the album, then we would chat, she would ask questions to which I would reply. After the first chat we had, she then said to the listeners, "We are going to play another track from Bill's recording then continue talking about his life with Van Morrison."

As the song played she turned towards me. "Don't be preaching," she said. I don't believe I was preaching, so I whispered a silent prayer in my heart to God, words such as, *Lord, what have You brought me here for? Was it not to let the people know what You have done for me and You can do for them?* I could see no better reason for me being there but to share the truth of God's love in sending His Son Jesus Christ to die on a cross to reconcile us to Himself.

When the song finished she thanked the listeners for tuning in and reminded them that she was Gloria Hunniford for BBC Northern Ireland.

The second half of the broadcast became heated when in my answer to a question she asked, I referred to the darker side of rock music (heavy metal) and spoke of the change Jesus had made in my life. At that point of the interview *Gloria got all shook up* and went for me like a dog barking at someone who had taken the bone it was chewing. I suppose even the best of broadcasters can have an off day.

As I drove home disappointed at how the interview had gone, the thought came to me of the words Jesus spoke to His disciples. *"If the world hates you, you know it hated Me before it hated you. If you were of the world, the world would love its own. Yet because you are not of the world, but I chose you out of the world, therefore the world hates you"* John 15:18–19, NKJV. I prayed as I drove, "Father, sometimes I feel I want to strike back — to hurt those who've hurt me, and this is one of those times. Help me display like Jesus a heart of gentleness and compassion."

"Christ went by the cross to the crown, and we must not think of going any other way." Matthew Henry, theologian.

I received a more gracious response from Eamonn Holmes, another Northern Ireland broadcaster who has enjoyed a successful career in broadcasting and television.

On the night Ozzie Osborne, the heavy metal, mixed-up-crazy little English guy who is supposedly to have bitten the head off a bat at one of his rock concerts, came to East Belfast Leisure Centre to perform, Eamonn Holmes, with an entourage of people bearing cameras and microphones arrived at our home in Banbridge. They had invited me and Ozzie to the UTV studios in Belfast where both he and I would go head-to-head in an interview with Eamonn Holmes, but Ozzie refused. Perhaps because there was no money in it, or he was afraid of being exposed as a fraud. I don't believe Ozzie bit the head off any bat; it was all a stage act to grab a cheap headline. So, I was asked if Eamonn could interview me at our home. It went very well, and after the interview we sat down together while the team gathered the equipment they had brought for the interview and put it into a van.

As he relaxed, we chatted about life and how he was trying to lose weight and trim down. It doesn't take much to be nice to people no matter how famous one appears in the eyes of the general public — this was Eamonn Holmes.

Candy Devine from Cairns, Queensland Australia was a lovely woman who was a broadcaster on Downtown Radio for many years before returning to her homeland of Australia.

I remember her saying as we talked on her radio show, "You've found the perfect package Bill, you've returned to your roots in music and found inner peace."

On September 30, 1995, *The Belfast Telegraph* wrote an article about the time I turned my back on the rock music scene after I came to faith in Jesus Christ and went into the pastoral ministry:

"PASTOR BILL'S CHANGE OF TUNE GAVE *VAN THE MAN* HIS SHOWBIZ BREAK.

Van the man replaced Bill Dunn, pastor of an Elim Church in Belfast, as lead vocalist of early 60s band *the Gamblers* a few months before they changed their name to *Them*. But Bill had already decided a lifestyle of liquor and late nights wasn't for him."

Van Morrison took my place after I left in 1964.

Later, on May 9, 2013, *the Belfast News Letter* also featured an article:

"The last band Bill played for was a band named *the Gamblers* who reformed under the name *Them* after he left. It was at that point, Van Morrison took his place as the fronting vocalist and within months got to the British pop charts with the song, *Here Comes The Night* and *Baby Please Don't Go*. With success like this under his belt, it's possibly not surprising that the young Bill Dunn began to live something of a rock 'n' roll lifestyle."

By Noel McAdam

A SINGER who lost out on a rock career to Van Morrison has returned to east Belfast — as a church minister.

Van the Man replaced Bill Dunn, pastor of Elim Pentecostal in Dundonald, as lead vocalist of early 60s band the Gamblers a few months before they changed their name to Them.

But Bill had already decided a lifestyle of liquor and late nights wasn't for him.

Now 52, he owes his Christian conversion to another rock'n'roll legend, however — Elvis Presley.

It was the King's rendition of the gospel standard Peace in the Valley which finally turned him from his self-confessed wicked ways.

"My life has come full

Minister hits own high note in city return

circle, really," he said.

"From the days of playing with the band to come back to the same area to try to work for God.

"I had been playing with bands since the early days of rock and roll around 1955, but frankly the drinking and so on was getting to me. We hardly ever walked on stage — we staggered on.

"The bottom line is that Van replaced me because he

was at a bit of a loose end. A few months later they were in the Top 20."

But Bill had by that time already swapped the beat for the Bible and the Charts for Christ.

"A lot of things were going on. A man who worked as a painter was ministering to me. But the crunch was one night when I put an Elvis gospel EP on.

"I always liked Elvis, used

to imitate him on stage, but there he was, the biggest star in the world at that time, singing Peace in the Valley and I realised that is what everyone is after in life," he said.

But it wasn't until 1971 that Bill became a pastor, then serving in a few Ulster Elim churches as well as England, Scotland and the Irish Republic.

"It's great to be back here, though and I would still be in touch with Van sometimes. But I couldn't answer whether he is a Christian or not," Pastor Dunn added.

He last had a lengthy talk with Morrison on religion a few months before the superstar released his duet with Cliff Richard, 'Whenever God Shines His Light', which went to No 1 in the charts.

Chapter Ten

"Who's that Knocking at My Door?"

(Song written by Pat Enright)

If I had £1 for every time I've been asked what it was like hanging around and growing up with Van Morrison, I would be a millionaire by now. And you could be thinking, why is Bill always referring to Van? It's quite simple, if your wee friend grew up and became a worldwide singer and musician and still continues all these years later to come and meet this wee man call Bill Dunn, one has to be grateful.

Let me tell you about my long-term friendship with Van.

Van was ahead of his time in the Northern Ireland rock scene and light years ahead of us, those who played alongside him. He has sold seventy million records and counting. This is something his critics fail to recognise and give him credit for — an East Belfast boy who made it to the top of a music career.

For those in the media who say he won't grant them an interview, perhaps if they left his private life alone and concentrated more on his contribution to music and the way the world has shaped him, they might find him more willing. In a rare interview with Anthony Mason, which you can check out on YouTube, Van says, "I'm an introvert in an extrovert business … I want to sing the blues." To sing the blues means to open oneself up to how one feels inside — it can be feeling sad and discouraged. The lyrics of the song *Singing The Blues* are: *Well, I never felt more like singin' the blues, cause I never thought that I'd ever lose your love dear, why'd you do me this way?* This could be the reason a number of people don't understand blues' singers.

Both Iris and I were invited as guests the night Van was conferred with the city's highest honour — *Freedom of the City of Belfast,* then in 2016, he was knighted for services to the music industry and to tourism in Northern Ireland — Sir Ivan George Morrison.

I first met Van prior to both of us coming into our teens. He was in the backyard of his house in Hyndford Street strumming a guitar in a skiffle group he was establishing. The old back door of the house that led inside was open and a crowd of kids were gathered round watching. As I walked over to see what was going on, he kicked the door shut in my face. "Who is that egit?" I asked. It wasn't long after this that we met and became the best of friends and have remained so ever since.

Since my conversion and coming to faith in Christ there have been several times when he and I have met for lunch, and may I say, Van is always quick to pay the bill.

I remember a time in the 1980s when I got a call to meet with him in the Clandeboye Country Club, in County Down. We spent several hours sipping coffee, talking about old times and spiritual things. I showed him a cutting I had from the front page of the Irish News which had a photo of him with the caption *Van the Man Is Searching For The*

Way. I asked him if it was true, and he said yes. Before we parted I gave him some Christian reading material and gospel songs I had recorded. Six months later, before Christmas of that year he released his *Avalon Sunset* album which is widely recognised as spiritual. It carries the song, *Whenever God Shines His Light,* a duet with Sir Cliff Richard, which achieved a high spot on the British music charts and was broadcast on Top of the Pops in 1989.

When I am asked by the media and people who come to my evenings of gospel praise and ministry if Van Morrison is a Christian, I always answer with a verse of scripture, *"The Lord knows those who are His"* 2 Timothy 2:19, NKJV.

Ten years passed before we met at the Clandeboye Country Club again. The group included Van and past members of *the Monarchs,* another band I left before they went on tour to Germany. It was something that didn't interest me. Jonsey on bass, lead guitarist Billy McAllen, Big Roy the drummer and me, were invited for a video shoot. Van wanted us to participate.

Bill & George (Jonsey) Jones friends to this day.

We had plenty of laughs about the olden days as we sat around drinking coffee, with some drinking something a bit stronger, chatting about the early days in the music business and past experiences together while we strummed guitars, sang songs from a bygone era while the cameras rolled for about three hours.

When they finally turned off the cameras, a question was put forward and a discussion began. The question was, "Why did God kill all those people in the Old Testament?"

Have you ever thought about that? I know I have. How can the God of love kill people in their thousands if not millions?

I knew someone was knocking on the door, curious about God. The answer that he was seeking is in Deuteronomy 9 (When you have time please read it) and also in the book of Numbers 33:50–55. God gives Moses further commands for the people of Israel before they enter the land of Canaan:

"Speak to the Israelites and say to them ... "but if you do not drive out the inhabitants of the land, those you allow to remain will become thorns in your eyes and thorns in your sides. They will give you trouble in the land where you will live. And then I will do to you what I plan to do to them."

Because of the immoral lifestyle, the evil and wickedness of the nations in the land of Canaan, God raised Israel to be a holy nation and to bring about change. Leviticus 18:24.26 says, *"Do not defile yourselves in any of these ways, because this is how the nations that I am going to drive out before you became defiled. Even the land was defiled; so I punished it for its sin, and the land vomited out its inhabitants. But you (Israel) must keep My decrees and my laws."*

God's holy righteous nature compels Him to judge sin, and anyone who is unwilling to repent of their sin will one day experience the wrath of God at the Great White Throne Judgement.[5]

The Gospel of Christ is good news, and God's love for us is great.

The Gospel of Christ affects the whole person — mind, heart and will. And it does this in that order. The mind is persuaded, the heart is moved, and the will is surrendered.

The second greatest force in the world is sin, it must be because it caused the death of Jesus Christ, which means the first greatest force in the world is love. God's love for us is so great it caused Him to send His one and only son to die on the Cross for the forgiveness of our sins, and to bring us peace with God. As John 3:16 says, *"God so loved the world that He gave His only begotten Son ..."*

---

5 Revelation 20:11-15.

Chapter Eleven
"Like a Bridge over Troubled Water ..."

(Song written by Paul Simon)

There are times in everyone's life when trouble looks us straight in the eye; it's then that we need a bridge that can take us safely across.

The Bible says, *"Man is born unto trouble as the sparks fly upward"* Job 5:7. Jesus also said, *"In the world you will have trouble ... but take heart, I have overcome the world."*

I know of several times in life when death reached out to take my life as if the devil was determined to stop me from accomplishing God's call on my life. In the midst of the valley of the shadow of death, Jesus was my bridge to safety, and I believe when my time finally comes to leave this world He will be the bridge over the troubled water of death and lead me through that dark valley the Bible names as the *king of terrors*. (Job 18:14)

When I was only seven, I fell out of the cab of a lorry on to a busy road full of traffic after forgetting to close the door.

Then when I turned nineteen, one cold November morning, on my way to work, a car collided with my Suzuki motorbike on the busy Holywood bypass just outside the front gates into Holywood Army Barracks. I was knocked unconscious and ended up in hospital where

I needed surgery for broken bones. That entrance has since been closed because so many accidents took place there.

While pastoring a church in the town of Banbridge I escaped being killed by an IRA (Irish Republican Army) car bomb, which took the life of an eleven-year-old boy named Alan McCrum, and caused heartbreak to his family and devastated the residents of the town. That day I had been visiting families from the church. My last visit was in the town of Lurgan and I had to drive back to Banbridge to place an advertisement in the newspaper before it closed for the evening. The advert was for a special outreach event we had planned for later that week. I parked my car and ran down a narrow street lined with parked cars that led into the town. It was 5:25 p.m. As I left the newspaper office I walked up the same street, then I stopped beside the parked cars to check my watch. It was 5:28 p.m. I ran back down the street hoping I could get into the Bible bookstore before it closed. I made it in time, but just as I put my hand on the door handle there was a deafening explosion.

When I went back outside and looked up to where the explosion happened I knew that I had missed death by sixty seconds.

There was the time I was on holiday at Santa Ponsa in Spain with Iris and our youngest son Jonathan. I went swimming in the sea — Billy the deepsea diver wearing a snorkel and flippers. I got so caught up with what I was seeing on the ocean bed I hadn't realised I was being swept out to sea because the current had caught me. It was only when a massive wave crashed over me and filled my snorkel with seawater and I lifted my head to catch a breath of air that I realised the danger I was in. I could see crowds of people on the beach enjoying themselves, but I was too far out for anyone to hear my cry for help.

I became exhausted as I tried to swim against the current. I knew that I was drowning and I cried out to God. Instantly, a giant wave lifted me, carried me and threw me on to a rock.

No university degree can help in times like this — only faith in God.

Jeremiah 33:3 has often been called God's telephone number, *"Call to Me and I will answer you, and show you great and mighty things which you do not know."*

No circumstance or demon from hell was going to stop Iris and I from obeying the call of God, but it would be several years before I would be sailing across to England to enter Elim Bible College, which today has the prestigious title Regents Theological College. The Lord had unfinished work for us to do at home.

Knowing one's purpose and potential in life is the most rewarding experience of being alive. It is a tragedy so many miss it. The late Dr Myles Munro, highlights this in his book *Potential For Every Day.*[6] "The wealthiest spot on the planet is not the oil-fields of Kuwait, Iraq, or Saudi Arabia. Neither is it the gold and diamond mines of South Africa, or the silver mines of Africa."

Though it may surprise you, the richest deposits on our planet lie just a few blocks from your house. They rest in your local cemetery or graveyard. Buried beneath the soil within the walls of those sacred grounds are dreams that never came to pass, songs that were never sung, books that were never written, paintings that never filled a canvas, ideas that were never shared, visions that never became reality, inventions that were never designed, plans that never went beyond the drawing board of the mind, and purposes that were never fulfilled. Our graveyards are filled with potential that remained potential — what a tragedy.

The moment we make Jesus Christ Saviour and Lord of our life the potential He puts within us is valuable to the world, and we must decide if we are going to bless the world with it, or keep it to ourselves and locked away to take to the grave with us.

---

6 Destiny Image Publishers, INC P.O. Box 310 Shippensburg, PA 17257-0310

Chapter Twelve

"Burning Bridges Behind Me ..."

(Song written by Walter Scott)

After I was saved I immediately threw myself into Christian work. I believe in the old saying, *nailing your colours to the mast*. So, with a handful of gospel tracts, I stood at the corner of Bloomfield Avenue where it meets Newtownards Road and it wasn't too long before word was out on the streets, *Billy Dunn's got religion!"*

They were wrong, I hadn't got religion, all religion has done for the world is divide it. Jesus didn't come to start a new religion. He died on the Cross and rose from the dead to bring us into the right relationship with our Creator to enjoy the blessings of God in this life, and eternal life in the life to come.

I sold my guitar and equipment with the intention of never singing again even though it was what I worshipped and loved. But God had other plans for me to sing the life-changing message of the Cross.

One evening, a young city missioner named Desmond Ayr from the East Bread Street mission hall, a street near to where I lived, called to visit my mum. The City Mission do tremendous work offering that personal touch to people's lives as they visit the community offering essential pastoral care. A pastor, who is like a shepherd, knows how to care for his sheep and protect them from wolves and any who seek to devour them.

Christ did not call us to relate to the world, He called us to communicate unashamedly the good news of the gospel, which is the power of God to all who believe for salvation.[7]

The famous ship, *the Titanic,* which was built in East Belfast, was safe when it entered the water. It only became unsafe when water entered into the ship. Likewise the Church commissioned by Jesus to go into the world with the gospel is safe in the world, but is in danger the moment it forgets it's calling; it's then that the world gets into the church.

When he visited my mum, Des called at a time when I was at home and we talked about me singing and sharing my story at one of his Sunday night gospel meetings. I made every excuse to get out of it, but he was determined to get me there, which he finally did, and this was what brought me into a singing ministry where the Lord would open doors for me to record many CD's and DVD's of gospel songs and hymns. He also was one of several who mentored me towards the ministry that brought me into evangelism and pastoring as he took me with him on his daily rounds of door-to-door visitation and gave me opportunities to help around the mission hall.

At the Tuesday night prayer meeting I was a young Christian and I badly wanted to pray openly as others would be doing., Earlier, during my work day, while I had been painting the inside of a house, I promised the Lord and prepared myself inwardly to pray at the meeting. But immediately before the meeting I was scared, and I couldn't think what to pray for. But when the time came, and as one after the other rose to their feet to pray interjected with praise for the Lord and amen, I jumped to my feet and began. There was silence in the meeting when they heard a new voice; the voice of a young Christian praying. Amid the quietness, I heard my own voice praying, and with that I sat down as quickly as I'd stood up. I think this is the problem with many who would love to pray openly but are afraid — the fear of hearing their

7 Romans 1:16.

own voice and thinking that people in the meeting are listening only to them. I overcame this fear when I convinced myself I wasn't there to impress anyone; I was there to intercede with God on behalf of the lost, the lonely, and for those breathing their last breath who were about to enter eternity and meet God without having Christ as their Saviour and Lord.

They say an army marches on its stomach, well God's Army of Christian's march on their knees. In all the churches we pastored and watched grow in spirit and numerically we emphasised two things the Church of the first century put in place over all else, *"We shall give ourselves continually to prayer, and to the ministry of the Word"* Acts 6:4, KJV. The prayer meeting has become the Cinderella of the Church, the least attended meeting of all.

Someone quipped, "Seven days without prayer makes one weak."

On one of the days we were out together on visitation going door to door in the streets that were lined with terrace houses I spoke to Des. "I feel God is calling me for the ministry," I said.

"If God wants you to go to China don't stay in Northern Ireland, but if God wants you in Northern Ireland don't go anywhere else," he replied.

He even suggested the Bible college in Glasgow where he had studied and trained. Later, Des left the City Mission off the Lisburn Road to enter the Ministry of the Presbyterian Church. He died quite young but accomplished in his short lifetime what God had called him to do.

For a while I taught Sunday School at another mission hall — Windsor City Mission in Lisburn Road where I made many new friends, including some who helped bring me to another level in my walk of faith and preparation for ministry. There was Jimmy Steadman who had a great library of Christian books and took me under his wing and suggested what books I should read. Every Saturday he drove me to Christian bookshops around Belfast where the best second-hand books could be bought cheaply. Then there was Stanley Johnston, who later became a pastor and Bertie White who got me involved in street evangelism where I handed out gospel tracts and engaged in open-air preaching. Stanley had me singing and sharing my story.

I remember one Saturday at an open-air meeting; it was a summer night and the pubs were emptying out. The church Iris and I were attending was on Newtownards Road at the corner of Dee Street where there are now murals on the walls of the ship that sank on its maiden voyage — *the Titanic.* Joyful praise and singing could be heard along those streets that lead to the once famous Belfast Shipyard. As I was singing a Jim Reeves song, *In A Land Where We'll Never Grow Old,* such a large crowd gathered that they began pushing to get off the road and onto the footpath to get nearer. They came so close that I could smell the stench of alcohol from their breath. They stood listening; several with tears streaming down their cheeks. I have often wondered how many from that crowd made it into that land where we'll never grow old.

Stanley was the one to give me my first encouraging push towards preaching. He didn't ask me but told me he wanted me to preach at the forthcoming Sunday School prize-giving in two weeks' time.

Over the next two weeks I studied and worked hard on my sermon and wrote it on ten sheets of foolscap paper. *That will keep me going for at least twenty minutes or more,* I thought. But when I stepped on to the platform that Sunday night and saw the crowd that had gathered my twenty minutes was reduced to seven.

I grabbed my Bible notes and quickly sat down, but Stanley, without blinking an eye, picked up where I had left off and continued preaching on David and Goliath. He was one of life's unique characters, someone who loved and served the Lord wholeheartedly along with his wife, Helen. Stanley Johnston left this world and went to heaven in March 2022, the date God promoted him to glory.

Chapter Thirteen

"Thank You for the Music ..."

(Song written by Benny Andersson and Bjorn Ulvaeus)

Once I turned my back on rock music and was singing for the *Rock of Ages* — Jesus, the guitar began to open up more as if God Himself was now my teacher; new chords and rhythms flowed through my veins. Doors began to open; invitations came flooding in to share my story around the province as one church after another invited me. I have learnt along the journey of life that whenever I hand my life over to God and surrender to His will, He makes a better job of it.

In the church Iris and I had been attending, the pastor asked if I would start a gospel group. From that emerged *The Evangels*. Jimmy then decided to go to Bible College (1970), leaving Bobby and I. It was the following year that I went to Bible College which ended *The Evangels* in 1971.

The Evangels (from left) Jimmy Ritchie, Bobby Rice, Bill Dunn

Together with two other young men, Jimmy Ritchie on guitar and Bobby Rice on bass, we formed a Gospel group and it wasn't long before we were being invited all over Northern Ireland. Up until that time the only two instruments used in a church service were organ and piano, but things were about to change. We were one of the first to introduce electric guitars and bass guitar in church meetings and the people received this with open arms.

Once upon a time, I thought churches were boring and only for those whom life had passed by. I discovered that there was, in fact, much to do, many things to get involved in and so many events to go to, although some events had their moments and were not the highlight of the week.

I remember the time a group of my church friends were talking about a theologian who was coming from England and would be at the apostolic church in Great Victoria Street. I had never heard the word theologian before and it got me thinking it was a musician who played a melodeon (a small accordion) so I signed up to go. That night we climbed into the old church mini-bus. On the way someone said, "he's long-winded you know." I though he must have played a wind instrument such as a saxophone. Later that night I discovered how long-winded he was; I went in with short hair, came out of that meeting needing a hair-cut.

"A short speech requires great preparation; a long speech can be given anytime on short notice," said Abraham Lincoln.

It is of no surprise when I read of the drop in church attendance today or why some people have never darkened the door step of a church building. It is of little interest to the man or woman struggling with family problems, health issues, or the guilt and shame of sin how much Biblical knowledge the preacher has if he can't communicate in the language of the common man and point him to where he can find an answer and the cure for his problems — the Cross. Jesus never told his disciples to feed my giraffes. He said, *"Feed My sheep."*[8]

---

8 John 21:17.

Chapter Fourteen

"Follow that Dream ..."

(Song written by Fred Wise)

If you want your dream to come true, someone said, "You have to get out of bed and go to work, and work at it every day for the rest of your life."

Five years had almost passed from that night I heard the call of God to go to Bible college and train for the ministry. Iris and I had been invited by friends to the old YMCA Hall in Wellington Place, Belfast to hear an America preacher named Billy Graham preaching at one of his city-wide gospel crusades.

Who was Billy Graham? Everyone became so excited; you would think he was a Hollywood movie star or a rock star.

That night sitting on the third row from the front in a seat near the aisle I realised why my friends were excited. As I watched and listened, I was riveted to my seat. Then the preacher from the screen looked directly at me, or so it seemed, and he pointed his finger. "God is calling you," he said in a commanding voice.

It was only three months since I'd been saved, but that call never left me. Preparation is highly important and must not be entered into lightly. "I will prepare myself and someday my chance will come," said

Abraham Lincoln, and it finally did. After years of disappointment, he was elected as the 16th president of the United States of America in 1861 and is regarded to be the greatest president to ever sit in the White House. Bible College is a short time to spend preparing for a lifetime of ministry. So in 1970, after leaving Iris and my four year-old-son Paul to live with my mum, I headed for England and arrived later that day at the Bible college along with other Irish students, Tommy McGuicken, Jimmy Ritchie, and Raymond Cotter. After leaving Bible college, Raymond went on to become a very successful pastor, then later he took on the role of missions director for the Elim Churches in Ireland. During his time there and even when he retired he raised thousands of pounds for overseas missions.

The Bible says, *"God is not unrighteous to forget your work and labour of love which you have shown toward His name"* Hebrews 6:10.

The Irish students had to stay to the end of each term which lasted three months because it was too expensive to fly back and forth from England to Northern Ireland during mid-term break. Unlike the English, Welsh and Scottish students we didn't have a government grant to help towards our college fees. We had to raise the money ourselves. Iris and I paid the first-year's fees by selling the car and all of our furniture. Iris continued working while my mum looked after Paul during the day. Then in the summer months when I was home, I looked for employment and saved this for the following year's fees.

It was during this time that our home church, the Ulster Temple on Ravenhill Road encouraged us greatly when our Pastor David Ayling, told us that the church was going to help us financially with next year's fees.

In my last term at college I had an experience that was a miracle. At the request of Pastor Archie Biddle, I was sent to his church to assist with ministry. It was a large congregation at Portsmouth Elim. I was given a ticket for the train and told he would call me on my arrival at the train station at 8 p.m. I arrived well within the time and waited outside three phone booths for either one to ring, but no call came. I waited until 8.15 p.m. then 8.30 p.m. When it came to 8.45 p.m., I had become anxious. I couldn't make any calls because I had not brought any loose change with me as I'd been told that the pastor would call and arrange to pick me up.

As I paced back and forth outside those three phone booths that stood side by side I felt the urge to go into one in particular.

I knew that would be useless; I had no money to make a call, and then I found myself walking into one as if someone had taken me by the elbow and led me inside.

Sitting in the slot was a ten pence coin, just enough to call Pastor Biddle. Some will say the 10p coin was left by mistake, forgotten by someone who was making a phone call. That may be so, but whoever it was, God got involved and made that person leave it for one of His servants who was going to need a miracle. Over the years I have seen and experienced the fulfilment of that wonderful promise of Philippians 4:19, "But my God shall supply all your need according to His riches in glory by Christ Jesus."

Bill and Iris being awarded Bachelor of Arts degree in Bible/Theology, 1994

After Bible college I continued studying towards a Bachelor of Arts degree in Bible/Theology, which I was awarded on August 11, 1994, while pastoring a church in County Monaghan.

Our first church was in the north-east of England, the Elim Church in Bishop Auckland.

The meetings were held in an old Methodist church building and in the winter months we had to wear extra-warm clothing because, for some strange reason, the old gas heaters were sited halfway up the walls of the building. The pigeons that came in through the loft above were nearer to the heat than we were. They perched on the metal rafters. This meant they were given more attention than my preaching. They kept the congregation on the edge of their seats as they watched, anxious to avoid any showers of blessings they didn't want to receive.

Our next church was in Scotland in a town outside Glasgow named Kirkintilloch. The work of a pastor is more than preaching sermons, choosing hymns and spiritual songs and planning special events to keep everyone together. I discovered very early on that in pastoral ministry you have to help and deal almost on a weekly basis with people going through hurt and damage. Just a few months after arriving at Kirkintilloch, I was asked to conduct the funeral of a baby. I had previously officiated at funerals but that was for older members at the church in the north-east of England — this was different.

In their house I met the young couple who were in floods of tears; it was their first baby, a baby girl born with spina bifida who lived only three weeks. The girl's mother who came to the church we were pastoring had asked me to conduct the funeral. I held a small service in their home then we all waited outside while the baby's father climbed the stairs to the bedroom where the body lay. As he came out of the house my eyes caught sight of what he was carrying — a small white coffin the size of two shoe boxes. My heart broke for them as I held back the tears. Revelation 21:4 says, *"God shall wipe away all tears from their eyes; and there shall be no more death, neither sorrow, nor crying, neither shall there be any more pain; for the former things are passed away."* But until that day comes, a pastor is called to minister and comfort those who weep and are broken-hearted.

Of course the joyful and happier moments in church ministry far outweigh the unhappy times. There is nothing more exhilarating and uplifting for a church and for the pastor when people are being saved; when some diamond in the rough comes to faith in Jesus and joins the church.

In several of the churches we were leading almost every Sunday night we saw people coming to faith and being set free from all sorts of problems and vices.

I remember two brothers who were saved. The night they we being baptised I asked them to share a brief word of testimony. The oldest one made the congregation roar with laughter when he said, "This pastor doesn't know, but before he came to this town I worked on this church. I was on the roof stripping the lead."

The younger brother was married; he and his young wife were expecting their first child. About six months later I received a phone call at 2 a.m. in the morning. I grappled for the phone which almost fell out of my hand because I had been in a deep sleep.

"Is that Pastor Dunn?"

'Yes," I replied in a tired voice.

"We have a young man here who says he's a member of your church. His wife has just given birth, and there have been complications; the baby's head is swelling and this young man is panicking and out of control. Would you come to the hospital please?"

I went into the bathroom and threw water on my face then got dressed.

The life of a pastor — one moment you're laughing, the next you could be sitting beside someone whose life is falling apart and crying with them. Only a fool would want to be a pastor, one who was not called by God.

Then there were the husband and wife who were well known in the town for their wild parties and things unmentionable. One night at a baptismal service, which always brought in a large crowd of people, I got them both to share with the church their conversion story.

The husband started by saying, "Mary and I were into the iron and steel business. But since we've both been saved the business has closed down." A deathly silence came over the meeting. But that quickly changed to laughter. "Mary did the ironing and I did the stealing. We have since closed down that business," he added.

It is always a great joy to conduct a wedding and bring two young people together as husband and wife. Counselling and helping them with advice, not, of course, the advice a nervous young girl was given on her wedding day. One particular bride's mother said, "Now Mary, when you walk into church tomorrow remember these three things, aisle, altar, hymn, and keep repeating that over." And she did, but she misunderstood the words. She interpreted it as *I'll alter him.*

The Lord gives us these special visitations for He knows every pastor at some time will experience disappointment with some in the congregation who are quick to judge their motives for leadership. Jesus had to deal with this often. Mark, chapter three, opens where the Great Shepherd Jesus is again in a synagogue. Sitting before Him are some who are there only to find fault with what he would do. The Bible says, "... *would he heal a man with a withered hand on the Sabbath day?"* When He had looked round about on them with anger, being grieved for the hardness of their hearts, He said to the man with the withered hand, *'Stretch forth your hand.' And he stretched it out; and his hand was restored whole as the other"* Mark 3:2,5, KJV.

Pray for your pastor, the one responsible for feeding and leading the church. Pray the Lord gives him much grace and wisdom, and be slow to point the finger as there will be three from your own hand pointing back at you.

Chapter Fifteen

"I'm Still Standing ..."

(Song written by Elton John and Bernie Taupin)

During our time in Scotland, we believed God would soon call us back to Northern Ireland, which he did in 1977, to a problem church that was split.

I discovered early on in our ministry that there were some strong personalities who were grieving the Spirit of God and who were a hindrance to the work of the church. Someone put it like this, "There are too many chiefs here, Pastor Bill, and not enough Indians."

For over a year I preached, I visited, I prayed and held special weekend gospel events but nothing exciting was happening. I then turned to prayer and fasting, which I did for twenty-one days and drank only water. The body can go without food for many days, but it can't go beyond three days without water because it will dehydrate. At the end of the year on Old Year's Night just before the New Year at our Watch Night service, which was an open meeting for the members to share what the Lord had done for them over the past year and what they hoped God would do in the year ahead. In my message to the congregation, I challenged them. "This new year let's believe the Lord will add seven new families to our church fellowship," I said.

The spirit of doubting Thomas was very evident. But at the end of that year more than seven families were added at the next Watch Night service where one of the Deacons spoke, "Last year when our pastor asked us to believe and pray people into this church I couldn't see it happening, but here tonight I have been proven wrong."

As the church grew we had to add a gallery to the old building to house the crowds that were coming because of the numbers who were being saved. We arranged for plans to be drawn for a new building.

Some years later while I was on holiday at the Isle of Man, God told me that our time was finished at that church. We would be moving to another town, to Banbridge, the town where Joseph Scriven who wrote the famous hymn, *What A Friend We Have In Jesus,* was born. This was another church where we saw God moving in signs, wonders and miracles as people were being saved, set free from sin and finding God's purpose for their lives. I used all means I could think of to reach the anxious heart, the broken heart and the sinful heart. I held gospel missions and crusades both in the church building and outside in large canvas tents in the town. These lasted three and four weeks, with preaching and singing every night. Saturday was a rest day for the new week starting on Sunday. These meetings drew large crowds and lives were changed. The same as at our previous church the congregation grew and we had to extend the building.

1969

Recognition has to be given to the men who guarded the tent every night. Each of them took their turn sleeping in a caravan near to the tent while another watched. This was during the height of *the Troubles* in Northern Ireland. Some had to go to work the next day after staying up long hours. I was so grateful to the ones who made the church such a blessing and a success to the glory of God. The Lord knows each of them by name.

On a cruise ship while hundreds of holiday-makers are enjoying the voyage only the captain and a handful of officers are visible on the bridge and these are the ones who get all the praise. But it's the crew below deck who keep the big ship operating and the stewards who serve that determine the ship's progress for most of the voyage. And in the local church the same principle applies; it's the engine-room crew and stewards who serve faithfully and carry out much of the work that determines the success of the witness and ministry: caretaking staff, Sunday School teachers, youth workers, bus drivers, car park attendants, the visitation team, the prayer warriors. While high-profile people tend to get most of the applause and the rest go unnoticed God reserves a special recognition for the below-deck crew. And if you're one of them, one day in heaven you will hear His public announcement, *"Well done, good and faithful servant! You have been faithful with a few things; I will put you in charge of many things. Come and share your master's happiness!"* Matthew 25:21.

Chapter Sixteen

"I'm a Believer"

(Song written by The Monkees)

I believe there is a solution for every legitimate problem, no matter how difficult the problem appears to be. Life's experiences have taught me that whenever I come to the end of myself, I arrive at the beginning of God. And God has always made a way where it seemed there was no way. Every prison door has a key, every river has a crossing point, every mountain will have a tunnel, ask for it, look for it, search for it, listen for it. Those who attempt the absurd can achieve the impossible. Jesus put it like this, *"If thou canst believe, all things are possible to him that believeth"* Mark 9:23, KJV.

There are some who confuse the word *belief* with the word *wish*. The two are not the same. Everyone is capable of *wishing* for financial, material, or spiritual advantages, but the element of faith is the only power by which a wish can be translated into belief, and then what one believes becomes reality.

Many have been amazed at what they were able to accomplish once they replaced the wishbone with backbone by living out their faith publicly.

Iris and I were always willing to go anywhere — provided it was forward, and it is amazing where God will take you, if you are willing to follow.

So after several years pastoring at Banbridge, and witnessing development in both numerical and spiritual growth within the church body we moved from pastoring and entered a new sphere of ministry — full-time evangelism. This took a lot of travelling and meant being away from home sometimes for several weeks. The gospel is not something we come to church to hear; it is something we go as the church to tell a lost and dying world.

When you're on the road travelling alone miles away from family, friends and those who know you, you can't let your guard down and give a place to that sly old fox called the devil. Temptation is something we cannot escape, but something we can expect.

I was always conscious of the One who was watching, "You-Are-The-God-Who-Sees-Me."[9]

During a preaching tour of England, on the ferry across from Larne to Scotland and after parking the car onboard I headed towards the ship's restaurant. On my way I came to a slot machine. It brought back memories of a misspent youth.

I used to love playing those gambling machines. As I stood gazing at it I heard a sinister whisper, "Go on, have a go. You're on a ship; no one is going to see you." I'm glad I didn't because just as I walked away from the very spot the Superintendent of the Elim Churches in Ireland — Eric McComb walked around the corner. He had been elected that year as the president of the Elim Churches world-wide and was travelling to England to visit and minister at several churches on mainland Britain. We shared with each other the churches where we would be ministering, then parted company. Then I finally discovered the ship's restaurant, and to my surprise as I entered several voices spoke, "Hi Pastor Dunn, come on over and have a coffee with us." It was a group of about seven or eight men, prison officers from the Northern

9 Genesis 16:13 NKJV.

Ireland Prison Service. They had formed the *Prison Officer's Christian Witness* and were going to minister at several churches in Scotland. There's a little song which has the line, "His eye is on the sparrow, and I know he's watching me."

During my years as an evangelist the Lord opened new doors of opportunity. I was asked to write a weekly column in two Irish Newspapers — *the Northern Standard* and *the Cavan Leader,* and also a weekly broadcast on UCB Ireland and a television ministry on the gospel channel. I recorded several gospel albums on CD, and DVD, all while I was travelling throughout Ireland, North and South, and across to mainland Britain, to America and Canada, preaching as well as singing the life-changing message of the Cross.

"When we have you at our church we get a double whammy — a preacher and singer," one pastor who invited me to minister at his church said.

I have great respect and wonderful memories of the pastors and leaders of the many churches who opened their doors to invite me to minister the gospel.

Time and space do not allow me to mention each one by name. But there is one who stands out. Pastor David Williams was the minister of an Elim Church in Silverdale, a town in the potteries of England. The church started in an old pawn shop, but David's vision for the church led people to greater things, and I had the privilege of seeing that come to pass.

David invited me many times over the years to hold gospel crusades. During the day he had me singing and speaking at the schools in the area, then at night holding crusade meetings. These were exciting times, days of mini revivals. Each time I returned to Silverdale, I saw David's vision explode into reality.

It does not surprise me that today there is a large Elim Church building from where the leaders and the people they lead reach out into their community.

It's amazing to think that in that old pawn shop years ago, people with not very much means would take some item to pawn to raise enough money to help them through until next pay day, then later in the week return to the pawn shop and redeem *(buy)* the item.

When the church took over the pawn shop to use for their praise and worship meetings, redeeming was something the pastor and his congregation kept very much alive.

Visitors who came with their sin and guilt heard the story of God's Redemption — Jesus Christ dying on the Cross. And if they would believe and bring their sin to Him, they would receive forgiveness, for He died to redeem them. The words of a gospel song say it all, *He bought my soul through death on Calvary.*

One of Bill's many CD titles.

Chapter Seventeen

"Kung Fu Fighting"

(Song written by Carl Douglas)

In 1997 and 1998 I was invited to minister in New York City at the Rock Church Manhattan; for three weeks on both occasions.

On one of these visits I was asked to sing and share my testimony in Central Park at a large outreach arranged by a cross section of the churches in the City of New York. I didn't know anything about the congregation I was to minister to. It was a large crowd of drug addicts and derelicts who society had given up all hope of rescuing, but the Church hadn't. As I stood on the make-shift platform I said a prayer that I was getting through to the lonely and broken lives seated before me — many were smoking pot and getting high on drugs as I sang and preached.

On another occasion without support from any church, along with a handful of willing workers who had a passion to win souls and witness for Jesus, (God knows each of them by name and will reward them one day in heaven) I planned a large tent crusade in Craigavon near the Craigavon Lakes. The field was kindly loaned to us by the district council. This was quite a financial burden to take on. There would be the cost of hiring a large tent, advertising in the press and all other means possible to make the meetings known. So I brought it to God in prayer and put a cut-off date where I decided that if financial support

had not come in by a certain date I would accept it was not God's will at this time for such an evangelistic endeavour. I remember so well the Saturday morning of the cut-off date. I was kneeling at my bedside very despondent and about to say in prayer, *Lord, it must not be your will for this Gospel Mission to proceed so I will ...* At that moment the phone rang, I picked it up. On the line was a Christian business man from Portadown. "Hello Pastor Dunn, this is ... I hear you are planning a tent crusade at Craigavon Lakes."
"Yes," I replied.

"You'll be needing financial support for such a venture. I'm phoning to say whatever it costs I'll cover the bill."

That started a wonderful friendship and a means of support, as he and his wife unknown to anyone, blessed Iris, me, and our children during those years when I was on the road as an evangelist. I am not surprised that the Lord gave him success and enriched his business because there were many others he helped, such as missionary organisations to further the Kingdom of God. God's work done in God's way will never lack His provision.

There is a principal taught in the Bible, "If you give to God what is in your hand, God will give to you what is in His hand, and God's hand is bigger than ours. But not until we release what is in our hand will God release what is in His hand." *"Give, and it shall be given unto you, said Jesus, good measure, pressed down, and shaken together, and running over, shall men give into your bosom. For with the same measure that ye mete withal it shall be measured to you again"* Luke 6:38, KJV.

That business man, a faithful servant of God is now in the presence of Jesus.

I believe as he entered the gates of pearl in heaven, Jesus was there to welcome him with, *"Well done, good and faithful servant; you were faithful over a few things, I will make you ruler over many things; enter into the joy of your Lord"* Matthew 25:21, NKJV.

After several years of itinerant ministry, travelling thousands of miles each year by car, ship and plane, the Lord called us back to pastoring. Our last church was in the beautiful lake district of County Fermanagh to the village of Brookeborough, where again the Lord walked among us manifesting His power and blessing; souls were saved and added to the Church, and lives were transformed.

In and from the Brookeborough Elim Church we taught and led the people to reach out into their community with the *good news'* message.

In the words of the great Apostle Paul, "I have become all things to all men, so that I may by all means save some." I produced a gospel newspaper with testimonies and true-life stories of people in the church, and the varied events that happened each week within the church. It was delivered to hundreds of homes and dwellings, including several tent crusades, and special evangelistic meetings in hotels. We even hired the British Legion Hall in Fivemiletown for a five-night series of special gospel meetings which I named *Mission Possible.*

For fifty years or more, it has been my privilege to serve the Lord Jesus Christ and His church as a pastor and evangelist. I have many precious memories that I treasure, and there are also some I'd rather forget. But I would do it all again because of the eternal rewards that await in heaven, and because the one who stood alongside and encouraged me in the work of the ministry — my partner in life Iris, has already gone to receive her reward in heaven.

The work of a pastor can be satisfying and rewarding, but it can also be extremely difficult and discouraging at times as it drives you around disappointing bends on the road of life.

I remember well the late Reverend Tom Walker, one of my college lecturers, talking to the class on the topic of pastoral theology, "When you leave college and take up your first pastoral duties you will discover you are working with the hardest material in the world — human nature. A carpenter can shape wood, an iron-turner can twist and bend iron over a hot fire, but no one can turn human nature. Don't be disheartened; God's Spirit is there to help and work alongside you."

Among the churches Iris and I pastored I can think of names of songs that would suit some of those churches, for example, *Heartbreak Hotel, Kung Fu Fighting,* and *Please Release Me let Me Go.*

I smile about it now, but back then I had a number of sleepless nights until I read somewhere that when crows attack an eagle, the eagle soars higher and higher in ever-widening circles until the pests leave it alone. This is truly a great strategy for any pastor or leader of a church. I put it into practice early on in our ministry. In my devotional and quiet time with the Lord each morning, I soared above my critics instead of stooping down to their low level of living.

Isaiah 40:31 says, *"But they who wait upon the Lord shall renew their strength; they shall mount up on wings like eagles, they shall run and not be weary, they shall walk and not faint."*

It is always sad to hear of church splits and pastors resigning from the ministry, which it appears, is happening more today than at any other time in church history. For some, their pastor can't do anything right no matter how hard they try. There's always someone ready to find fault and criticise, such as the guy who said, *I can preach better than him.* Perhaps he could. He only preached two or three times a year. For a pastor he has two Sunday services to prepare for, a Bible study and prayer meeting during the week, along with the visitation of the sick and elderly.

I keep away from those who try and call me into their vendetta with the pastor. God's word says, *"Touch not mine anointed, and do my prophets no harm"* 1 Chronicles 16:22.

The great Pastor Moses with a church of two million couldn't please his congregation even though God gave him signs, wonders and miracles to confirm he was called of God to lead them.

On one occasion they were ready to stone him to death and threatened to go back to Egypt and suffer again as slaves.

Moses demonstrates the heart of a great pastor for his people.

Exodus chapter thirty-two records the event where Moses is on the mountain for forty days and nights fasting and praying for God's people of Israel and receiving commandments from God for them. Moses' brother Aaron made an idol to worship — *the Golden Calf.* The Lord told Moses he was going to destroy them because of this sin. Verse 31 says Moses went back to the Lord and said, *"Oh, what a great sin these people have committed! They have made themselves gods of gold. But now, please forgive their sin but if not, then blot me out of the book you have written."*

Pastors have a tough job not unlike a football manager who is only as popular as the size of the crowd and the result of the last few games. Pastors often get more kicks than kisses.

Someone described a pastor's life in the following way: If the pastor is young he lacks experience; if his hair is grey, he's too old for the young people. If he has five or six children, he has too many; if he has none, he's setting a bad example. If he preaches from notes he is dry and boring; if he doesn't use notes he is shallow and long-winded. If he caters to the poor in the church, he's playing to the gallery; if he pays attention to the wealthy, he's wanting a rise in salary. If he uses too many illustrations, he's neglecting Biblical depth; if he doesn't use illustrations, he isn't clear. If he condemns sin and wrong doing, he's old fashioned; if he doesn't preach against sin, they claim he's a compromiser. If he forcefully preaches the truth, he's too offensive; if he doesn't present the *whole counsel of God,* he's a hypocrite. If he doesn't please everybody, it's time he left; if he makes everybody happy, he has no convictions. If he drives an old car, he shames his congregation; if he buys a new one, he's setting his affection on earthly things. If he preaches all the time, the congregation gets tired of hearing the same voice every week; if he invites guest speakers, he's shirking his responsibility and wasting the churches finances. If he receives a large salary, he's mercenary and lacks spirituality; if he receives a small one — well, then they say it proves he isn't worth much anyway and should never have been called to be their pastor. This might exaggerate the situation, but nevertheless it emphasises an attitude found in so many churches.

I know a superintendent of a church denomination who was called to see a church session (church board) who were looking for a new pastor. After the usual greetings and deliberations, they handed him a list specifying the type of person they wanted.

After reading the long list of requirements the superintendent looked at them wearily and said, "I'm sorry to be the bearer of bad news gentlemen, the man you're looking for hasn't been born yet."

There's an old Arabian proverb which says, "If you stop every time a dog barks, your road will never end."

Peter, in his first letter writes, *"Shepherd the flock of God which is among you, serving as overseers, not by constraint but willingly, not for dishonest gain but eagerly; nor as being lords over those entrusted to you, but being examples to the flock; and when the Chief Shepherd appears, you will receive the crown of glory that does not fade away"* 1 Peter 5:2–3, NKJV.

Over the years, in the work of church ministry, I have found that there are three stages in every great work of God; first it appears impossible; then it looks difficult, but finally it gets done. If you keep drilling you will finally strike oil, so don't give up and don't give in. Believe you're on the brink of a miracle.

To anyone thinking of going into the pastorate of a church, go where you are celebrated not where you are tolerated. You might have to wipe the dust off your feet in some places and move on as Jesus said in Matthew 10:14, or dig in and remain faithful to where God has called you, in case there is someone whose head is up in the clouds thinking it's all about luck. Luck only happens when preparation meets opportunity. And I took every opportunity God gave me and proved that if I didn't give up but kept believing and working God would finally turn up. *"To everything there is a season, and a time to every purpose under heaven,"* says Ecclesiastes 2:1.

Pastors have responsibility. We care for the flock that God has given us to lead. Imagine two mountain hikers, one has a light back-pack while the other poor soul is loaded down.

It could be a long-standing grudge that is poisoning his insides, or a broken relationship with his wife or one of his kids. That heavy pack could be loaded with unpaid bills. The question is, where can they go to unload? Meeting with them in Starbucks for a coffee is not the right environment, sitting in church alongside a couple of hundred other folks is hardly the right place. What he or she needs is a place where there is a person who cares, where they will feel free, without embarrassment to open up and share what it is that is causing them to struggle. The pastor who says don't go after those who leave has never grasped the parable Jesus tells about the lost sheep where the shepherd left ninety-nine safe and went after the one that was lost.

Of course compassion alone does not move God to answer our requests. The world is full of needy people. If it was compassion alone in the heart of God that answered the cry for help He would visit every hospital, heal every sick and needy person, but the Bible says in Hebrews 11:6, *"Without faith it is impossible to please Him. Anyone who comes to God must believe He exists and that He rewards those who diligently seek Him."*

Chapter Eighteen

"Son of a Preacher Man"

(Song written by John Hurley and Ronnie Wilkins)

Who would want to be one? I mean what child wants to be a preacher's kid, the son or daughter of a pastor? They get picked on at school and called *weirdos* or *religious freaks*. If they retaliate they are regarded as hypocrites and could even be treated in church as the black sheep of the family.

Poor pastor and his wife, they need to take that child in hand; a good spanking would sort that one out. I have often felt sorry for the older couple in church who have never had a child to love and bring up; who don't understand the responsibility and problems that can arise both in and outside the home. They can be quick to give advice or complain to the pastor about a certain child who is noisy and unruly in the Sunday service. At times, these people don't think in reality. Perhaps they have never grasped or don't understand the words Jesus spoke as a rebuke to His disciples on the day that mothers brought their children to Jesus for Him to touch and bless, yet the disciples turned them away. When Jesus saw what was happening, He was displeased and said to them, *"Let the children come to Me, and do not hinder them, for the kingdom of heaven belongs to such as these."* Matthew 19:13–14.

I wouldn't be at all surprised if these kind of people judge the late Queen Elizabeth and her husband the late Prince Philip as failed parents.

The children of the royal family are often in the news and it's often about bad stuff. Out of the four children born to them, only one remains married to his original spouse — Prince Edward, the rest are divorced and some have remarried. I didn't hear calls for Her Majesty to abdicate the throne and to step down because of this. She had a magnificent reign of seventy years. What about King David, a man after God's own heart who was regarded to be the greatest king to reign on the throne of Israel?[10]

Even David wouldn't have had a ghost of a chance to remain as king of Israel according to some inward-looking people who believe that when he died, the truth died with him because of his domestic problems and problems with his children. "We can't tolerate this behaviour. One of his sons tried to kill him and take the throne while another raped his sister. Give him three months wages and let's look for new leader."

When the great evangelist of the 20th century, Billy Graham, was alive, hell would have frozen over before he would have received an invitation to speak at certain exclusive church events. All of Billy and Ruth Graham's children had struggles in their early life. Three of their children divorced while their sons Franklin and Ned turned to drugs. But they returned to the fold and all are now in ministry. In the story of the prodigal son recorded in Luke 15:11–32, Jesus does not cover over the sin of the prodigal, He talks openly about it while exposing the hypocrisy of the self-righteous older brother who was pointing the finger of condemnation at his younger brother.

Both of our sons, Paul and Jonathan know what it was to be a preacher's kid. Paul was seven and Jonathan had just been born when we pastored our first church in the north-east of England.

I am pleased to say that in all of the churches we pastored, our boys never had this problem. There were times when their halo's were a bit

---

10 Acts 13:21-22.

bent, but the people were understanding. They probably thought, *they're a picture of their dad, our pastor, they're daft as a brush but they'll grow out of it!* And yes they did, Paul and his wife Gail pastor a great church in Ballymena along with Pastor Mark Stone and his wife Melanie. My son Jonathan and his wife, Annette, are committed to Christ and are involved in a great church in Portadown. While my three grandchildren have all been saved and are serving Jesus. My oldest grandson Paul junior and his wife Anna are worship leaders in an amazing church at Fraserburgh in Scotland, while Andrew and Amy are involved in their local church here in Northern Ireland.

Paul and Gail

Jonathan and Annette

Paul, Anna and Joseph

Andrew and Amy

Chapter Nineteen

"Shine Your Light Against the Dark ..."

(Song written by Charlie Landsborough)

Out of the sixty-six books in the Bible, did you know that there is one book unfinished? It contains twenty-eight chapters and from the opening prologue to the final statement, it is action the whole way to the end.

I am referring to the book of Acts, the fifth book in the New Testament. J.B. Philips in his paraphrase names it: *The Young Church In Action,* a title worthy of all that is revealed within its twenty-eight chapters, a history of the 1st century church. I believe we, the Church of the 21st century are writing the final chapter.

In the opening section of the book, Luke, the writer communicates with a high-ranking official in Rome and gives him a thumbnail sketch of the birth and activity of the early Christian believers.

After being crucified, pronounced dead, and then buried, Jesus Christ rises from the dead and appears to His followers and informs them that they are now to be His witness to the world. Then He promises to send the Holy Spirit to empower them. He maps out God's outline for world evangelisation in Acts 1:8, which remains to this day, Jesus said, *"You shall be My witnesses in ... "*

JERUSALEM — The Difficult Place ...

Jerusalem was the home city of many of those early followers of Christ. It was difficult way back in the 1st century to be a witness, and things haven't changed today in the 21st century. Whether that be in your home church, your hometown, or the home and district where everyone thinks they know more about you than you know about yourself.

JUDEA — The Dangerous Place ...

It wasn't too long after the birth of the infant church that persecution started, first in Judea and then it spread very quickly to other places and scattered the believers like embers of fire all over the land. Time has not changed the way the world views a Bible believing Christian. It is reported that there have been more Christians martyred in the 20th century and up to the present time than in any other time in history. The Christian life is not a playground; it is a battleground, at this present time reports say persecution is on the increase around the world.

SAMARIA — The Dark Place ...

When Philip, the evangelist went to Samaria to preach the gospel, he encountered Simon, the sorcerer who had the city bewitched. Should we expect anything different today? I know there is a devil for two reasons, first the Bible declares it, and second, he often comes to tempt and try to discourage me.

Some years back in the late 1980s, I was invited to bonny Scotland by Mike Epton, the then pastor of the Elim Church in Edinburgh for a week of special salvation and healing meetings. The meetings went well with many people receiving God. On one of the nights I felt something strange in my spirit during the meeting; there was heaviness as I preached. I noticed a woman who had come for the first time. Near the end of the meeting she disappeared very quickly. After the meeting ended I walked to the door that lead into the street. As I opened the door to step into the hall she jumped out from behind the door and startled me. "Pray for me," she said. People were moving out, so I took her aside and asked her to bow her head. Jesus said, *"Watch and pray."*[11] So I did.

She was a large, tall woman. I watched as she bowed her head and closed her eyes. In that moment I witnessed something startling. Her eyes began to glow. It was as if from inside this woman a demon was standing over me, laughing, looking down and saying, *Who do you think you are wee man, you have no power over me?* My immediate thoughts were, *but Jesus has all power and authority over you.* At that moment the Spirit of God spoke this word into my heart. *"You are of God, little children, and have overcome them, because He who is in you is greater than he who is in the world"* 1 John 4:4, NKJV. As I took authority in the name of Jesus over what was happening the atmosphere quickly changed, as did the poor wretched woman. The Bible says: *"If the Son therefore shall make you free, ye shall be free indeed"* John 8:36, KJV.

THE UTTERMOST PARTS — The Distant Place ...
God's work done in God's way shall never lack God's power and God's provision. When I traced the history of the church recorded in the book of Acts, the growth was phenomenal.

Starting in Acts 1:12–15, prior to the Day of Pentecost the number of believers recorded is 120, although Paul records 500 men who had seen Jesus alive after He rose from the dead — (1 Corinthians 15:6).

On being filled with the Holy Spirit, the church quickly grew to 3,120, Acts 2:41. Then 5,000 believed and were added to the church. (Acts 4:4.) After this church growth was so phenomenal in size that Luke begins to refer to *"multitudes being added to the church"* Acts 5:14.

This is how believers in the 1st century did church, lived and witnessed for Jesus. Today in the 21st century we do church differently. We stand

---

11 Matthew 26:41, KJV.

in a building looking at a screen to sing songs, then we sit and listen to sermons and call it *A Celebration Service.* The 1st century believers didn't just have a celebration service in a church building — they took it outside into the market place to let the world know that they had something wonderful to celebrate and that the world needed to hear.

When I was saved in 1965, the people in the church I was attending used to sing, *Let me burn out for You O God, don't let me rust out,* and I used to join in singing those words with my eyes closed, and my face turned towards heaven. I meant it with all my heart, though it was probably more emotional than scripturally and doctrinally correct. As the years passed and I began to study the scriptures and grow in the faith, I discovered God didn't want me to burn out. He desired for me the same as He desires for every believer and follower of our Lord Jesus Christ — burn on, do not burn out.

God taught me this lesson one dark winter's night as I was travelling home late from a meeting in the country where I had been speaking and singing. Without warning, the outside lights on my car cut out and I was plunged into total darkness. The only way I was able to get home was by driving slowly and nursing the car along by using the hazard lights. That's when I heard God speaking into my heart about something I had read in Matthew 5:14–16, but the message came to me in this fashion, *The lights on a car are necessary to lighten up the darkness and the way ahead but are useless when not lit. For the length of time I have given you on this earth you are to be a light to the world. Let your light shine to show the way for those who walk in darkness. If you don't shine the light great will be the darkness many will be travelling along the journey of life.'*

Mother Teresa that little woman who did such remarkable work for the poverty stricken of India said, "I know God won't give me anything I can't handle. I just wish He didn't trust me with so much." The scriptural fact is, God will not give us more than we can handle but grace that will help us to handle the work that needs to be done. If you are doing more than God expects of you, you're heading for a breakdown.

Some years further on in my walk of faith, the thought entered my mind, *When I die what will happen to me?* I usually answered in the same vein. *I will go to heaven and will receive my reward for services rendered in this life. I will see my mum and dad, my wife Iris, and other loved ones who have been in heaven for many years.* But none of these answers brought any satisfaction, not until one evening while I was driving home from a large tent meeting where I had been ministering in County Armagh. The answer lit up in my head and I saw what it was. When I die, and when you die, all what we have will die with us. Those God-given gifts, abilities and talents will die with us. My singing ability will go to the grave with me, and the anointing God placed upon me to preach and teach His Word and explain the gospel will die with me, unless I pass it on to others.

Job is a man mentioned in the Bible who said, *"Naked I came into the world and naked I will leave it again"* Job 1:21–22. We came in with nothing and we leave with nothing. That was when the thought came to me of starting a school of evangelism to teach God's people around the churches how to witness and share their faith. Pastors and church leaders are obsessed with theology but are weak when it comes to explaining their faith in Jesus and teaching their congregation how to.

For what purpose is a head full of Bible knowledge or the best praise band in town if the people don't know how to communicate the gospel of Jesus Christ boldly and effectively? Sadly no one shared this vision with me.

In the book of Hebrews chapter twelve verse one we're informed of a race that every follower of Jesus Christ is in and we are exhorted to "run the race to the finish line." This race is not the one hundred metre sprint, neither is it the gruelling marathon often seen at the Olympic

Games. I believe the race the writer of Hebrews is referring to is the *relay race* where each contestant carries a baton and runs to the next person waiting in line ahead and passes the baton to them, and they in turn do the same to the next person waiting in line ahead; this goes on and on until the race is finished. Whatever ability or God-given gift you have, pass it on, don't take it to the grave with you. In Psalm 71:18 David prayed: *"Even when I am old and grey, do not forsake me, O God, till I declare your power to the next generation, Your might to all who are to come."*

E. Stanley Jones, the great missionary to India, wrote in the twilight years of his life; "When I get to heaven, I will ask for twenty-four hours to see my friends. Then I'll go up to my Master and say, 'Haven't You a world somewhere with fallen people, who need an evangelist like me?' Please send me there, for I know of no heaven beyond preaching the Gospel to people. That's heaven to me. It has been and it ever shall be."

The greatest form of praise is the sound of consecrated feet seeking out the lost and hopeless.

Our last chapter in life can be our best. Our final song can be our greatest. It could be that our whole life has prepared us for a grand exit. Don't go out in a puff of smoke; go out with the fire of God red hot in your spirit.

The term *Intelligent Design* is the mantra of the 21st Century church to a disillusioned world that has been brainwashed into believing *the Big Bang* Theory. Intelligent design means God created us to operate as He does. Genesis 1:26 says, then God said, *"Let us make man in Our image, in our likeness."*

I have been informed that the Hebrew word translated into the English word LIKENESS means *to operate like,* not just *to look like.* i.e. God's original design for us requires that we function like God which confirms all the more the words of Christ in John 14:12, NKJV, *"Most assuredly, I say to you, he who believes in Me, the works that I do he will do also; and greater works than these he will do, because I go to My Father."*

The Lord's message to the church in these last days before Christ returns is, "Don't give up; you're on the brink of a miracle."

Chapter Twenty

"I am Sailing"

(Song written by Gavin Sutherland)

Someone said that the Church is like a great ship passing through the vast oceans of time carrying passengers from the Old World to the New. On the journey there are times it seems we are sailing on a cruise ship because everything is so good, and everyone is enjoying the trip, then suddenly we find it's as if we are in a battleship engaged in spiritual warfare. With Jesus as captain we can rest assured we will arrive safely in that New World. While some of the crew are called to lead, we are all called to help to work together for the good of the journey.

Let's look at this journey through the eyes of a pastor which is a wonderful privilege with a great responsibility, as Jesus said, *"Unto whomsoever much is given, of him shall be much required: and to whom men have committed much, of him they shall ask the more"* Luke 12:48, KJV.

Pastoring a church is like being a ship's captain, a leader of people who plans for the whole trip not just for a Sunday cruise.

In his mind before they leave the dock, the captain has a clear vision of their destination, he understands what it will take to get there, he knows who they need as a crew for the journey to be successful, and he recognises there will be obstacles before they appear on the horizon, and some difficult hard-nosed people on board. The captain, who plans well in advance, can take his people just anywhere. If we want God to bless our plan as a leader of others we must have a plan He can bless.

Pastoring a church is not for the faint-hearted. In all walks of life secular or religious, sooner or later, a leader will meet the crab family and have to deal with them.

If you go into a fish market, laid out on slab you will find all types of fish for sale including lobster and crab. Under that table there will be a bucket with more crabs so when the crabs on the slab are sold the fishmonger reaches into the bucket and puts more out. While people are making their purchase the crabs in the bucket below are fighting to get out, walking on top of one another. If one makes it to the top of the bucket another one from below will reach up with its pincers and pull it back down and walk on it. It's the sad and sorry picture of what goes on in church and what is called the fellowship of the saints.

Over the years while I was pastoring churches I encountered a few from the crab family. I will mention one. There had been a new election of deacons and later that week as we gathered to discuss church business and plan for the way ahead, we had no sooner started than a newly elected voice cut across what I was saying. "I've been elected as the voice for the people in this church and I'm here to make their complaints known." Here was a guy it seemed who was comparing the working of the Industrial Trade Union to a church deacon's job. One of the older men at the meeting quipped, "Hold your fire brother, are you going to call for an all-out strike and hinder progress in this church?" Psalm 133 says, *"Where brethren gather together in unity it is there God commands His blessing."*

In the mid-1980s, I was invited by the Pentecostal churches of Canada to minister in some of their churches. I was in Toronto on a Sunday evening preaching and there was a great anointing on the meeting.

The following day being Monday the pastor took me out to lunch. While we were sharing thoughts on the previous night's service a man in his thirties entered the restaurant and the pastor waved him over and introduced me as a preacher from Ireland.

During the conversation I discovered he had been in the ministry but had left.

I always find it sad when this happens and I am interested to know why so many who train for the ministry later go back to secular work. So I asked him why? He looked sheepishly at me, then he smiled. "I couldn't roll with the punches," he replied. This is what a boxer trains for — to learn how to roll with a punch so he won't get knocked out. In the ministry one has to learn to overcome the punches of bullying, gossip, and even backstabbing. It's nothing new in the work of God.

Moses the Pastor of pastors and his brother Aaron, the high priest of Israel had to deal with the threat to their leadership from a number of hard-nosed people. The book of Numbers chapter sixteen is the record of the time Korah, with Dathan and Abiram, rose up to challenge them and said, "Why do you exalt yourselves above the congregation of the Lord?" Neither Moses nor Aaron had taken it upon themselves to lead Israel; it was God's idea. Exodus chapter four records the conversation between the Lord and Moses at the burning bush. Moses tried to excuse himself from taking on such a roll. So his and Aaron's leadership was being challenged, what did he do? He asked God to open the earth and swallow them up, which God did.[12] As we are no longer under law but now under grace, even though one may be tempted to use this method to remove a disruptive person it would not be advisable.

I came across a fable about a man who was given a parrot. When he brought it home the only thing the bird would say was, "I'm as hard as nails." This went on for days until the man got so weary listening

---

12 Numbers 12:15–33.

to it that he went out and bought a falcon and put both birds in a large cage thinking that the falcon would kill the parrot, but the next morning he found the falcon dead on the bottom of the cage and the parrot running back and forth along the perch screeching, "I'm as hard as nails, I'm as hard as nails."

The next day he went out and purchased a Harris Hawk and put it in the cage with the parrot. The same thing happened, later when he went back to the cage the Hawk was lying dead and the parrot was dancing on the perch like Mohammed Ali, flapping its wings and screeching, "I told you I'm as hard as nails."

In desperation he went out and bought a golden eagle — the king of birds, which makes its nest high on a mountain cliff; it can see for miles and even spot a small rabbit or a mouse.

He put the eagle in the cage with the parrot and left them. In the early hours of the morning there was a terrible commotion, a lot of squawking, rattling and banging coming from the cage. He thought it was the eagle finishing that pesky parrot. But when he went in to see, there was the eagle dead on the bottom of the cage, only this time the parrot had no feathers, it was naked. "What happened?" he asked. "That was a tough one you gave me this time," said the parrot, "I had to take my coat off to him." There are times in life when we have to take our coat off and deal with some strong personalities or else for the rest of our time we'll be a puppet on a string and not do what God sent us to do. There is a lot of truth in the saying, "When the going gets tough, the tough get going."

God told Joshua, who followed Moses as Israel's leader: *"Be strong and of good courage; for to this people you shall divide as an inheritance the land … have I not commanded you? Be strong and of good courage; be not afraid, nor be dismayed; for the Lord your God is with you wherever you go"* Joshua 1:6–9, KJV.

Chapter Twenty-One

"𝓛essons ..."

(Song written by Eric Roberson, Anikan, Vader and Jarius Mozee)

Life is all about *lessons,* what choices do we make and what do we learn from them? Here are some lessons I took onboard ...

I won't break if I bend ...

As a young pastor I wanted to learn as much as I could and as fast as I could so I began reading biographies, the lives of those who accomplished what they set out to do in life for the Kingdom of God, not just how and what they did, because I realised the key they had found that opened their community or their town might not be the key suitable to open the community where I was working and leading a church. I sought to learn from the flaws and mistakes they had made. One lesson was never to be obstinate, which helped me to avoid big waves that could have drowned me before I got started.

There's an old maritime legend about the aircraft carrier whose obstinate captain almost caused a disaster at sea. The story may or may not be true, but it illustrates the point that in order to be a successful leader one must be willing to change course when necessary to avoid sinking the ship. I know of several churches that at one time were doing well; whereas today they look like a shipwreck.

The captain of an American aircraft carrier was called to the bridge where he was alerted that there were lights approaching them on a collision course.

He immediately had a message sent telling the approaching lights to divert their course 15 degrees to the north. The response he received was, "We recommend you divert your course 15 degrees to the south to avoid collision." The captain was affronted in front of his crew and immediately barked the command, "This is Captain James Burrows of the Aircraft Carrier USS Abraham Lincoln, the second largest ship in the United States' Atlantic fleet. We are accompanied by three destroyers, three cruisers and numerous support vessels. I demand that you change your course 15 degrees north. That's one-five degrees north or counter measures will be undertaken to ensure the safety of this ship.

There was silence while they waited for a reply. The following message came through, "This is Fred Jones, I have been the keeper of this lighthouse for the past twenty years, I would strongly advise you to divert your course, captain." Learning the facts instead of jumping to conclusions gets the job done successfully.

Sometimes the leader has to eat humble pie. The Bible says, *"God resists the proud, but gives grace to the humble … humble yourselves in the sight of the Lord, and He will lift you up"* James 4:6,10, NKJV.

Expect the unexpected …
God called Abraham to follow him without giving him a map or a compass for the journey ahead. Because Abraham followed and expected the best, he got the very best God would provide. No one knows what the Lord has planned for us; we're just asked to trust and follow His lead. Like a man named Fleming.

He was a poor Scottish farmer. One day, while trying to make a living for his family, he heard a cry for help coming from a nearby bog. He dropped his tools and ran to the source of the cry. Mired to his waste in black muck, was a terrified boy, screaming and struggling to free himself. Farmer Fleming saved the lad from what would have been a slow terrifying death.

The next day, a fancy carriage pulled up at the Scotsman's sparse place of abode. An elegantly dressed nobleman stepped out and introduced himself as the boy's father.

'I want to repay you,' said the nobleman. 'You saved my son's life.'

'No I can't accept payment for what I did,' said the Scottish farmer, waving off the offer.

At that moment the farmer's son came to the door of the family hovel.

'Is that your son?' the nobleman asked.

'Yes,' the farmer replied with a smile.

'I'll make you a deal. Let me take him and give him a good education. If the lad is anything like his father he'll grow to be a man you can be proud of.'

And that he did. In time, farmer Fleming's son graduated from St Mary's Hospital Medical School in London, and went on to become known throughout the world as the noted, Sir Alexander Fleming, who discovered penicillin. Years later when the nobleman's son was stricken with pneumonia it was penicillin that saved his life. The name of the nobleman was Lord Randolph Churchill; his son's name was Sir Winston Churchill.

Whatever is in your heart and mind to do for the Lord that will benefit others, let me encourage you with these words, "Don't give up you're on the brink of a miracle."

Daily refresh the mind ...
"Be not conformed to this world, but be ye transformed by the renewing of your mind, that ye may prove what is that good, and acceptable, and perfect, will of God." Romans 12:2, KJV.

Every plague God sent to Egypt mocked their gods. For instance, the Egyptians worshipped a goddess with a head of a frog, so God caused the land to be overrun by frogs. Finally, the Pharaoh called Moses.

"I give up," he said.

"When do you want me to get rid of the frogs?" Moses asked.

Pharaoh's response was classic. "Tomorrow," he replied.

Why not now, why wait until tomorrow? It has been said often that procrastination is the thief of time. Why then do we procrastinate? Maybe we're fearful because we don't know what changes will entail, or maybe we are just like Pharaoh, stressed out and anxious and have lost focus on what is important and going on around us.

At the end of each day I have found it a good practice to have a daily catharsis of the mind. The same as a computer, if we download too much junk we'll crash. We all need a daily clean and clear out — junk in, junk out. Time with God and resting each day is a priority for our spiritual health. Doing productive work is satisfying to our spirit. Serving God and helping other people is essential to fulfilling God's purpose for us, but it is easy to become so over focused on the here and now and so busy that we get so stressed out and could fail to see that rest and leisure aren't wasted but important for refreshing the body, soul and mind. Even Mohammed Ali who is regarded to be the greatest heavyweight boxer of all time had to take a sixty-second rest sitting on a wooden stool between each round.

In the Church there are those who say that the devil never takes a holiday, so neither should we in the work of God; they should remember that we are not supposed to imitate the devil; our example to follow is Jesus.

The Bible records the accounts of the disciples who Jesus gave authority over evil spirits and the power to heal the sick. They were excited about everything that they had seen and accomplished. Knowing that they were near to burnout Jesus said, *"Come aside by yourselves to a deserted place and rest awhile."*[13] For there were many coming and going and they did not even have time to eat.

Mental illness is talked about more today than at any other time in history. Psychologists and psychiatrists seeking the cause of it often treat it through therapy and medication. The Bible has a cure that has no side effects.

Every morning when I arise from sleep I open my Bible and pray that the Holy Spirit will give me his illumination to help me to hear the voice of God and understand what He is speaking into my heart as I ponder situations in my life.

Now we have received, not the spirit of the world, but the Spirit who is from God, that we might know the things that have been freely given to us from God.[14] The mind governed by the flesh is death, but the mind governed by the Spirit is life and peace.[15]

In Exodus twenty-three verses ten to twelve God gives the command to let the land rest every seventh year to recuperate from what it has

13 Mark 6:31 NKJV.
14 1 Corinthians 2:12 KJV.
15 Romans 8:6 NIV.

given out over the previous six years, and for humankind to rest every seventh day. But we think we know better than God. This is the 21st Century, the generation that never sleeps. We have television twenty-four hours a day, non-stop, 365 days a year, and shops that work around the clock twenty-four-seven.

By cramming too much activity into too little time we set ourselves up for stress. Like a guitar string that's pulled tighter and tighter, we end up snapping, and then feel guilt, thinking we've let the Lord down.

God's answer before we reach burnout or blow up is, *"Come ye yourselves apart into a deserted place and rest awhile"* Mark 6:31, NKJV.

If we don't come apart and rest common sense says — we will finally come apart.

Know the season I am in ...
Autumn, winter, spring and summer, each of the seasons of the year serve their purpose on planet earth for it to safely spin and provide us with all we need for living. *"To everything there is a season, and a time to every purpose under the heaven"* Ecclesiastes 3:1, KJV.

Five minutes from where I live is a plantation that provides me with a pleasant walk. I have walked this almost every day with my little dog Sorcha since coming to live in Bangor, and I have discovered the seasons never alter or change their cycle. The Creator has given them an assignment: *"While the earth remaineth, seedtime and harvest, and cold and heat, and summer and winter, and day and night shall not cease"* Genesis 8:22, KJV.

There have been times when there were different voices clamouring for my attention. If I had listened to them I would have been greatly distracted from my assignment and purpose in life. Those distracting voices did not come mainly from the world, but there were voices also from the church.

When Iris and I had decided that I should go to Bible College a Christian friend said to her, "Are you sure about what you're doing? This might be a foolish decision. You're happily married and comfortably well off."

It is important to be sure in our minds and hearts what God has called us to do; what our assignment is. If you are not sure there are people out there who will think for you and quickly give you their opinion, so be careful little ears what you hear, for the Father up above is looking down on us in love, so be careful little ears what you hear.

"Brethren," writes Paul to the church, "I count not myself to have apprehended: but this one thing I do, forgetting those things which are behind, and reaching forth unto those things which are before, I press toward the mark for the prize of the high calling of God in Christ Jesus. Let us therefore, as many as be perfect, be thus minded" Philippians 3:13–15, KJV.

Like Paul, having God's assignment has been my obsession and motivation.

Everything God created is a solution for a problem. Mothers solve emotional problems. Dentists solve teeth problems. Lawyers solve legal problems.

Every person I know has two in them. What I mean is we are either part of the problem or part of the solution. The reason why there are unsolved problems in the world is that many do not know their assignment — why God put them here, what problems they can solve; many fail to fulfil their God-given assignment.

Your assignment on the earth is to solve a problem for somebody somewhere and receive a reward for it. A clockmaker named Peter Henlein is credited with inventing the very first watch — the watch serves a purpose. In 1886, Karl Benze patented the first motor vehicle known today as Mercedes. We who drive know too well the purpose the motor car serves. A compass is a helpful bit of kit.

It was first invented in China during the Han Dynasty between the 2nd Century BC and 1st Century AD and today in the 21st Century it serves a purpose.

They used to be called binmen or dustmen; today they are waste disposal operatives. It doesn't matter what name they go under, when I see them driving that big lorry down the street and the men busily emptying the waste bins, they are as important as a brain surgeon. Both have a different salary, but they each help solve a different problem.

Early on in my Christian walk something began to stir within me, I believe the Spirit of God was leading me to my life's assignment which I embraced over fifty years ago and I'm still enjoying the journey.

Ways I Seek to Discern God's Assignment?
I Decide Not To Enter Into What God Has Planned For My Future While Still Living In The Past.

Twenty years from now most people will be disappointed by the things they didn't do. Proverbs 23:7 says, *"As a man thinks in his heart, so is he."* "We are what *we think* about all day long," said Ralph Waldo Emerson.

Early on in a church Iris and I were pastoring I saw there was a mindset that was holding back this great enterprise we call the *Church of the Living God.* No matter how much I tried confronting it no one wanted to be disturbed.

In all walks of life there are some people who don't want to be all shook up; they are content being *"at ease in Zion"* as Amos 6:1, KJV, says. The problem it presents is, God doesn't infuse a fossilised mind with fresh ideas.

The story is told of a minister, who after years of seeing no change in his church, was afraid to leave; he began visiting the train station every day to watch the *twelve-noon flyer* go through. He was asked why. "It's the only thing that moves in this wee town that inspires me," he replied.

"I will never enter into what God has planned for my future while still living in the past," falls into the category of the great apostle Paul's message to the Church. *"Forgetting those things which are behind, and reaching forth unto those things which are before, I press toward the mark for the prize of the high calling of God in Christ Jesus"* Philippians 3:13–14, KJV.

"Death and life are in the power of the tongue" Proverbs 18:21, NKJV; which means, our own words can have more power to influence us than anyone else's words. Be in control of your thoughts and don't let anyone mess with your head.

I Believe What God Assigns Me To Is For The Benefit Of Others.
Joseph was sent to Egypt as a slave who later saved North Africa from starvation. Genesis 50:18–20. Philip, the evangelist was sent to the city of Samaria *to set it free* from the power and influence of satan. Acts 8:5–13. Jesus *had to go* through Samaria to meet *a greatly troubled woman"* John 4:4, KJV.

What Grieves Me May Be A Clue To What My Assignment Is.
While he was in captivity, Nehemiah understood this when he received heart-breaking news about his homeland Israel ... *"The wall of Jerusalem also is broken down, and the gates thereof are burned with fire. And it came to pass, when I heard these words, that I sat down and wept, and mourned certain days, and fasted, and prayed before the God of heaven"* Nehemiah 1:34, KJV.

What makes you weep and cry may be a clue to the problem God is calling you to fix.

What I Love Doing Most Could Reveal A Hidden Gift Within Me.
Simon Peter was an experienced fisherman. After a night of fishing, he came back to shore with his fishing nets empty. The next morning Jesus met him. "Follow Me, and I will make you to become a fisher of men," he said.

I Will Only Succeed When My Assignment Becomes An Obsession.
The Bible Book of Ruth is the story of a Moabite girl who was an alien to Israel. It's a rag to riches story showing what we can achieve if we set our heart and mind to it. From the opening chapter of the book through to the final chapter we see one girl's obsession that led her to success far beyond her wildest dreams.

After losing everything that was dear to them, Ruth said to her mother-in-law, *"Entreat me not to leave you, or to turn back from following you: for wherever you go, I will go; and wherever you lodge, I will lodge; your people shall be my people, and your God, my God. Where you die I will die, and there will I be buried. The Lord do so to me, and more also, if anything but death parts you and me. When she saw that she was determined to go with her, she stopped speaking to her."* Ruth 1:16–18.

From an early age in life I have been conscious of keeping fit and healthy and more so when I came to Christ and read that my body was the temple of the Holy Spirit who dwells within me, and in every follower of Jesus.

There are those, of course, who look for an excuse to avoid the *no pain no gain mentality* and quote 1 Timothy 4:8 in their defence, *"Bodily exercise profits little."* Implying that if there is little benefit in it why do it at all?

Every personal trainer will almost always say before you finish the workout and the cool down period, "Come on, finish strong," for they know that the human body has a tendency to want to slow down or draw back after it's been in motion through strenuous exercise.

Watch a horse race. The first horse and jockey out of the gate won't win the race if they don't finish strong. As they approach the final run to the winning post the jockey uses the whip as he spurs every ounce of strength from the horse.

The writer of the New Testament book Hebrews adds this to the theme of the book when he writes, *"Therefore we also, since we are surrounded by so great a cloud of witnesses, let us lay aside every weight, and the sin which so easily ensnares us, and let us run with endurance the race that is set before us"* Hebrews 12:1, NKJV. Jesus Himself wills us to finish strong. *"No man having put his hand to the plough, and looking back* (draws back) *isn't fit for the Kingdom of God"* Luke 9:62, NKJV. I find it interesting if not challenging that Jesus uses the word *fit,* for the Kingdom of God.

It is very easy to find a reason for drawing back and not pressing on. The Bible character Job is an example of all who don't draw back but finish strong.

Having lost everything, family, finance, and friends through no fault of his own, he gets up from the dust and cries out in faith, *"Though He slay me, yet will I trust in Him."* Chapter forty-two of his book records how greatly he was rewarded, see Job 42:10–17, NKJV.

Through all that the apostle Paul suffered for the gospel he could have found reason to draw back, but he didn't. If he had done he would have missed the amazing experience of being caught up to the third heaven, and seeing and hearing things no other living mortal has seen or heard. When you get some free time read and meditate on 2 Corinthians 11:18 through to Chapter 12:7.

I'm sure like me, as you draw near to the finish line you'll want to finish strong.

Probably the greatest example in modern times of persistence and finishing strong is Abraham Lincoln. If you want to learn about somebody who didn't quit, look no further.

"The sense of obligation to continue is present in all of us. A duty to strive is the duty of us all. I felt a call to that duty." Abraham Lincoln.

Born into poverty, Lincoln was faced with defeat throughout his life. He lost eight elections, failed twice in business and suffered a nervous breakdown.

He could have quit many times — but he didn't and because he didn't quit, he became one of the greatest presidents in the history of the United States of America.

Lincoln was a champion who never gave up. Here is a sketch of his journey to the White House, starting in year 1816.

1816   His family was forced out of their home. He had to work to support them.

1818   His mother died.

1831   He failed in business.

1832   He ran for state legislature and lost.

1832   He also lost his job — wanted to go to law school but couldn't get in.

1833   He borrowed money from a friend to begin a business and by the end of the year he was bankrupt. He spent the next seventeen years of his life paying off the debt.

1834   He ran for the state legislature again and won.

1835   He was engaged to be married, but his sweetheart died and he was left heart-broken.

1836   He had a nervous breakdown and was in bed for six months.

1838   He sought to become speaker of the state legislature but was defeated.

1840   He sought to become elected but again was defeated.

1843   He ran for congress and lost.

1846   He ran for congress again, this time he won and was sent to Washington and did a good job.

1848   He ran for congress and lost.

1849   He sought the job of land officer in his home state and was rejected.

1854   He ran for the senate of the United States but lost.

1856   He sought the vice-presidential nomination at his party's national convention and got less than 100 votes.

1858   He ran again for the US senate and lost.

1860   He was elected president of the United States.

After losing a race for the senate Lincoln said, "The path was worn andslippery, my foot slipped from under me, knocking the other out of the way, but I recovered and said to myself, it's a slip and not a fall."

God's Word to us is, *"Be strong and of good courage"* Joshua 1:9, KJV.

After all these years, we're still friends.

Chapter Twenty-Two

"When a Child is Born ..."

(Song written by Fred Jay)

The birth of a child can bring great joy and happiness to a family. As shared in the first chapter, if you're of a certain age there were no video cameras in that day, then none of us will really remember what took place. Did our parents cry with joy or say gosh, are you sure that's my child? I, like you, will never remember who held me, did they smile or not, what did they say about me, but do you know God knows us before anyone knows us? Scripture says, *"When my bones were being formed, carefully put together in my mother's womb, when I was growing there in secret, you knew that I was there — you saw me before I was born. The days allotted to me had all been recorded in your book, before any of them ever began"* Psalm 139:15–16, GNT.

The world hopes and many pray for a child to be born who will bring the world together in peace and harmony, sort out the mess no world leader seems to know how to do. One key we all hold, you and I can either help sort out problems or help make them, so God tells Jeremiah, you've been set apart ... why? Because we have been authorised by God to be helpers of God.

"Before I formed you in the womb I knew you, before you were born I set you apart ... " Jeremiah 1:5, NIV.

The song, *When A Child Is Born,* recorded by the late Johnny Mathis expresses this ...

A ray of hope flickers in the sky,
a tiny star lights up way up high
All across the land, dawns a bright new morn,
this comes to pass when a child is born.

In the song Mathis has a monologue where he expresses this as he rambles out the words:

And all of this happens because the world is waiting,
waiting for a child, black, white, yellow, no one knows.
But a child that will grow up and turn tears to laughter,
hate to love, war to peace and everyone to everyone's neighbour.
And misery and suffering will be words to be forgotten forever.

I would be surprised, even shocked if before he died, Johnny Mathis didn't know that such a child was born 2,000 years ago in the little town of Bethlehem of Judah — God's Son, Jesus Christ was born. In the gospel of Luke it says, *"The angel said to her, Do not be afraid, Mary, for you have found favour with God. And behold, you will conceive in your womb and bring forth a Son, and shall call His name JESUS. He will be great, and will be called the Son of the Highest; and the Lord God will give Him the throne of His father David. And He will reign over the house of Jacob forever, and of His kingdom there will be no end"* Luke 1:30–34, NKJV.

An old Christmas Carol puts it like this, "The hopes and fears of all the years are met in Thee tonight."

Every new-born baby is a gift from God to the world, to live out a purpose and have a meaningful life. This is why abortion cannot be right. Every time there is an abortion the world is robbed of the hidden potential and God-giving gifts within that unborn child.

It's difficult to understand your surroundings and remember what was happening in life when you were just a baby in the arms of your mother; I wonder how the baby Jesus felt. He was human like us with the human limitations we experience as babies, yet He was God in the flesh.

There is only one real Jesus — God in the flesh and we are not him, but every new born baby is a gift from God to the world, to live out a purpose and a meaningful life with a destiny that will bring about change for the good and betterment of the world, either small or great. Have you ever asked, Why did God create me, what has God planned for my life? *"I know the plans I have for you,"* declares the LORD, *plans to prosper you and not to harm you, plans to give you hope and a future"* Jeremiah 29:11, NIV.

In *What the World Owes to Christians,* Dr Victor Pierce, an Oxford scholar, shares the story of the typewriter. The typewriter was a forerunner to the modern word processor. But how did a Christian come to invent it? To write sermons? Seriously! Christopher Sholes was concerned about his pastor who'd been busy all week visiting victims of an epidemic, comforting the bereaved and conducting funerals. Consequently, he had no time to write his Sunday sermons.

One day Sholes was discussing with a friend what could be done.

"It seems a pity there isn't some quick method of writing for busy folks like parsons," he said.

"Why not invent a machine?" his friend asked.

"I'll try," Sholes replied.

That rainy afternoon was the beginning of months of hard work. Finally, a group assembled one day to see him tap out on paper, in capital letters, C. LATHAM SHOLES, NOV 1867. Six years later Remington's recognised the typewriter as something that could revolutionise business. In those days business was mostly run by men, but the Young Women's Christian Association started offering courses in typing for women. Initially it created a scandal, but as the first typists to be trained were women, employers rushed to hire them. Hence the typewriter. The YWCA determined that a woman's place was not only at home, but could also be in the office. God's plan for Christopher Sholes was to be an inventor. You also are in God's plan, the question is, have you found it and are you following it? The Bible says, *"A man's heart plans his way, but the Lord directs his steps"* Proverbs 16:9, NKJV.

Chapter Twenty-Three
"The End of the Line ..."

(Song writer Bob Dylan, George Harrison, Jeff Lynne, Roy Orbison, Tom Petty)[16]

Paul Anka wrote the song, *My Way,* which was made famous by Ol' Blue Eyes, Frank Sinatra and also recorded by Elvis Presley. *And now the end is near, and as I face the final curtain. My friend I'll make it clear I'll state my case, of which I'm certain. I've lived a life that's full. I travelled each and every highway and more, much more than this, I did it my way.*

Elvis Presley died leaving everything behind for others to divide among themselves. After his death, many asked how much he left. "Everything, he could take nothing with him into the afterlife," someone replied. The Bible says in Job 1:21, *"Naked came I into the world, and naked shall I leave it again."*

In the mid-1980s, it was rumoured in several newspapers across America that before Frank Sinatra died he offered the Vatican a large sum of money if they would arrange an audience with Pope John Paul II to hear his confession. I don't know what truth there is in the story, but it is an awakening call that no matter what success we achieve in this life and claim, *I did it my way,* we leave all our accomplishments behind us to go into eternity unsure.

---

16 Jeff Lynne, Roy Orbison and Tom Petty.

Ancient scholars, Jerome and Tertullian referenced stories of how in ancient Rome, after a general triumphed in an epic victory, he was paraded on top of a gleaming chariot along the capital's central thoroughfares from dawn to sunset amid the roars and cheers of the people who lined the streets. The general basked in the adoration, and revelled in the greatest honour of his life.

However, legend has it that a servant stood behind the general for the entire day, whispering into his ear, *Memento mori.* (Remember you will die) Amid all the adulation, the general desperately needed humility that came with remembering that he was mortal.

Mortality is what makes each and every one of us equal; we are mortal, and when we reach the end of the line we will die. Woody Allen quipped, "I'm not afraid to die, I just don't want to be there when it happens."

In the oldest book in the Bible there is a question we all at some time think or ask, *"If a man die, shall he live again?"* Job 14:14, KJV. The Bible answers a big YES. "God has set *eternity* in the human heart." See Ecclesiastes 3:11, NIV.

When I was a child in primary school around the age of eight, like other kids of my age I often daydreamed. On one occasion after reading a children's story about a wizard who could make powerful potions, I told my mum and dad I wanted Santa to bring me a chemistry set for Christmas.

On Christmas morning there was my special gift. I just couldn't wait to get the box open. Inside were coloured liquids, powder, glass tubes and an instruction book. By late afternoon through trial and error I learnt how to make several things, invisible ink, stink bombs and other items. But what a disappointment, they weren't anything like the potions that the wizard in the book had produced. *If only he was my teacher in school,* I thought, I would ask him to teach me everything he knows.

Imagine a group of children studying astronomy. They are reading about the first mission to the moon and ask the teacher all sorts of questions about space. One child raises his hand to get the teacher's attention.

'What is the moon like?' the child asks.

The teacher is hesitant and lost for a conclusive answer simply because they never have been to the moon.

At the next astronomy class the teacher invites astronaut Neil Armstrong as a guest speaker. He looks at the boy who asked the question.

'Now, ask Mr Armstrong your questions about the moon. He is the man who walked on the moon. He's been there and came back to tell us what he knows.'

Jesus knows everything about life now and the life hereafter. He lived in heaven, came from heaven to earth, died on a cross, then rose from the dead so that all who will believe in Him and receive Him as their Saviour and Lord can have eternal life and live with Him in heaven forever.

John 17:1–2, records Jesus praying. And as He prays he refers to the time he came from heaven to earth, *"... Father, the hour is come; glorify Thy Son, that Thy Son also may glorify thee: As thou hast given him power over all flesh, that he should give eternal life to as many as thou hast given Him."*

And this is life eternal, that they may know thee, the only true God, and Jesus Christ, whom thou hast sent. I have glorified thee on the earth; I have finished the work which thou gavest me to do. *"And now, O Father, glorify thou me with thine own self, with the glory which I had with thee before the world was"* John 17:5.

Jesus has unrivalled knowledge about heaven, of all that happens in heaven, and He wants to share heaven with us. Yes, there is life after death.

Dr Elisabeth Kubler-Ross MD, from Flossmoor Illinois, a leading authority on death and dying, and Dr Raymond Moody Jr, are two well-known psychiatrists, who examined the case histories of over five hundred people who came back to life after being pronounced dead by their physicians. Their research convinces anyone with an open mind.

The people in the study described either a location of beauty, marvel, joy or peace, or they described something dreadful. And although their bodies were real, they reported floating outside of their body. After being confirmed *dead*, some who were blind were able to see. They talked about people who came into the room, what they looked like, and what they did while they were there. Yet when these people were brought back, the ones who were blind could no longer see. In his book *Life After Life,*[17] Dr Moody writes, "A doctor told me of his experience in attending a man who had been pronounced clinically dead. He succeeded in resuscitating the man, who then sued the doctor for bringing him back into this miserable existence from the glory he had experienced. One woman, described her situation after she had suffered respiratory arrest, reported that the doctors who tried to resuscitate her were pounding on her body as they tried to get her back while she looked down, and said, "Leave me alone.""

This age old question: "If a man dies, shall he live again" is answered by Paul in his letter to a young preacher named Timothy, *"The gospel according to the power of God, saved us and called us with a holy calling, not according to our* (religious) *works, but according to His own purpose and grace which was given to us in Christ Jesus before time began, but has now been revealed by the appearing of our Saviour Jesus Christ, who*

---

17 Author, Raymond A. Moody. Publisher, Mockingbird Books.

has abolished death and brought life and immortality to light through the gospel" 2 Timothy 1:8–10, NKJV.

The road of life is laid out before us and every day we walk this road either God's way or our way. Along this road of life we come to where the road divides in two and find we have to decide, shall I continue on the road marked *my way* or change and walk the road marked *God's Way?*

Life without God is like an unsharpened pencil — it has no point.

No one wants to walk through life and at the end be a loser. We all want to live life to the full now and then enjoy the eternal rewards at the end of the line.

The instruction that we follow will determine the future we create. Many a one who has sought to climb their own make-shift ladder to heaven, on reaching the top discover the ladder has been leaning against the wrong wall — it's then that they will be all shook up.

In the tenth century, Abd al-Rahman III was the ruler of Cordoba, Spain. After fifty years of a successful reign beloved by his subjects, dreaded by his enemies and respected by his allies he took a deeper look at life, "Riches and honours, power and pleasure, have waited on my call," he said of his accomplishments.

"But as I count how many days of genuine happiness I have had they amount to just fourteen. "O man!" al-Rahman concluded. "Place not thy confidence in this present world."

I decided to do this in May 1965 — *not to place my confidence in this present world.* This brought me to where I don't really care what anyone thinks of me, which is dangerously close to something everyone desires, the thing called freedom.

Over the years, every now and then God challenges me, and it's usually when the flame of enthusiasm is beginning to burn low, suddenly there's a spark that rekindles the flame within.

I had a project in mind that I believed the Lord wanted for a church, but I was finding it difficult to get two of the leaders to catch the vision. I was at the crossroads of either giving up or signing up for the long haul.

One evening while I watched the movie *Schindler's List,* I was greatly inspired. The film tells the story of one man's efforts to make the most of a desperate situation. As a director of a munitions factory in Poland, Oskar Schindler decided to use his position to save Jewish lives, by employing them in his factory. Schindler rescued many condemned Jews from the gas chambers. But keeping them employed was costly, and little by little he liquidated his personal property to keep his business afloat. At the end of the movie, the Nazis are defeated, and the full impact of Schindler's efforts is revealed as the dead are counted and the living stagger back to freedom.

There was one particular scene which inspired me. As Schindler knelt by the railroad tracks that had carried thousands to their deaths, he had a startling realisation. He could have saved a few more. Overwhelmed with regret, he lamented keeping the few personal assets he still owned. If only he had known when the war would end, he could have *done more,* but by then it was too late. This is what really challenged me. It reminded me of an old gospel song, *By and by when I look on His face (Jesus), beautiful face, thorn-shadowed face. By and by when I look on His face, I'll wish I had given Him more.* I did not want to let this happen. I believed with my heart the vision God gave me for the church and I was ready to see it through.

Two of the leaders resigned, one of them left the church with his family and joined another church, which was a disappointment as they were a good family and he was a great asset around the church. Forgiving those who hurt or disappoint us doesn't mean we approve of their actions. It means we are letting go of the past and journeying into a better future.

Within that year we saw several new families join the church, and within twenty-four months the church outgrew the building.

Oskar Schindler was a hero. He is credited with saving more Jews during World War Two than any other single person. Yet all he could think about was what he *didn't* do. He wished he had done more.

I've been journeying through this world for many years now, still actively preaching and singing about Jesus and the power of His Cross, ready to go when the phone rings and the person on the other end asks, "Are you free to come to our church to minister sometime. What date would suit you?"

I've preached the gospel from the streets of Belfast to the streets of Broadway, in Manhattan, New York and have seen its power to all nationalities and peoples and its effect to change lives.

As I get nearer to the end of the journey, in my heart, a great light shines a calm assurance for the future, *It is well, it is well with my soul.* How have you been getting on with your own personal life's journey? Have you felt for some time that you have lost your way and are you wondering what is the right road to take? Perhaps life for you has been like someone trying to navigate their way with a map and a compass in a mountainous area. You must choose which way to go, which route would be the quickest and the safest way home.

Would you rather make that decision alone, or would it be more helpful if you had someone who can put you back on the correct road — the road that leads you to a home in heaven and to eternal rewards? Jesus is the navigator who waits for you to ask for His help. Jesus said, *"I am the way, the truth, and the life. No one comes to the Father except through Me"* John 14:6, NKJV.

I have learnt that whatever life takes from us, The Lord can restore. He may not give us exactly what we want, but He will give us what is best.

Many are hindered in coming to faith in Christ through the idea, *what about the years I have wasted, the opportunities I've squandered, and the mess I've made of my life. I would be ashamed to offer the butt-end of my life to God now, I think He wouldn't be interested?* That's one of satan's best mind games, messing with your head. That same thought entered my mind often until I finally shook it off, and like snow on a ditch, it melted away.

It's in such times as this that God is the only one who can give hope.

The Bible says, *"Behold, the LORD'S hand is not shortened, that it cannot save; nor His ear heavy, that it cannot hear"* Isaiah 59:1, NKJV.

God's promise to anyone who has wasted their years and comes to Him in faith is, *"I will restore to you the years that the locust has eaten ... the consuming locust ... and you shall eat in plenty and be satisfied, and praise the name of the LORD."* Joel 2:25–26, NKJV.

The moment we exchange our plans for God's plans, replace our way of living for God's way and surrender our will to God's will, we are acting like Jesus who prayed on the night before His death, *"Father, not My will but Yours be done."* Jesus sacrificed all so we could live a full life — *"a life more abundant."* John 10:10.

He sacrificed having a home, a reliable income and social acceptance. He travelled a great distance from heaven to earth to share with us God's love, God's plan and purpose for living.

Ultimately, Jesus gave up His life to free us from sin, death, and hell. He set the example and shows us how to live God's way, so don't let people or problems define you; that is God's prerogative.

There are two airports near the city of Belfast. The George Best City and Belfast International, and I have used both quite often. From the city centre to Belfast International Airport the route is straightforward. All one has to do is follow the signs and ignore the distractions. As you leave Belfast take the M2 and drive until you see the airport sign. There is a slip road that brings you on to a straight dual carriageway and on to a large roundabout. If you have your GPS Satnav switched on it will tell you to take the second road which is straight ahead towards Templepatrick. As you drive straight through you will come to another roundabout; you take the road ahead which brings you to yet another roundabout where the road to the left leads to Craigavon and the road to the right leads to the town of Antrim. Don't be distracted; take the road straight ahead and within minutes you will arrive at Belfast International Airport where you will get wings that will lift you heavenward to your destination.

If there were no roundabouts on the journey to contend with, the road you're travelling on would be straight. Jesus said, *"Strait is the gate, and narrow is the way, which leadeth unto life, and few there be that find it"* Matthew 7:14, KJV.

Imagine your life is over and your obituary is published. What would you like it to say? What changes might you make now? Or, what distractions do you need to ignore to *finish the journey* well?

We all have a personal story to tell. At the end of the line, many are hoping they will be able to look back and say with pride, *I did it my way.* It would be eternally better for them if they got all shook up by a God experience and decided to do it *God's way.* In our hand, a pound will never be worth more than a pound, a dollar will never be worth more than a dollar, or a euro will never be worth more than a euro. Our life is of far greater value than any of these world currencies. If we sow our life into God's Kingdom, it begins a harvest we will reap for all eternity.

Chapter Twenty-Four

"Don't Give Up..."

I have been asked many times over the years about a gospel song I am well known for and asked to sing it almost everywhere I minister — *Don't Give Up, You're On the Brink of a Miracle.*

During the 1980s, which saw death and destruction continue across Northern Ireland as republican terrorists kept up their insane death wish towards the people of Northern Ireland, I was on one of my mission trips to Canada and had been away from home for three weeks preaching and singing, by invitation of the Pentecostal Churches of Canada.

One evening after I returned to where I was staying I was tired and weary and I sat down with a cup of tea and switched on the TV. As I flicked across the channels, I happened to come upon some Christian broadcasts. This was long before the UK and Europe had such broadcasts on any of their networks as they have today.

I was drawn to a small group of believers who were singing. As I listened to the words, *Don't give up you're on the brink of a miracle, don't give in God is still on the throne.* The Spirit of God spoke these words very clearly into my heart. *Take this song back to the people of Northern Ireland.*

Shortly after arriving home, I recorded the song and taught it everywhere that I ministered. Although it became known as Bill Dunn's song, it's not my song, I didn't write it. I just obeyed what I believe the Lord told me to do. *Take it back with you to the people of Northern Ireland.* Through this simple act of obedience, I have seen people encouraged, helped, healed, saved and blessed.

Here is one out of many examples how a simple act of obedience to God sends out ripples.

Recently, I attended the funeral of a dear friend who loved Jesus and served him with all his heart. After the funeral service in the church we all gathered for light refreshments. As I stood in line with others an excited woman came across.

"Pastor Dunn, I have some wonderful news to share with you."

I'm always ready for *good news* as there is too much negative news being pumped into our heads. She introduced herself then told me the good news that had her so excited.

"Some time ago my husband fell seriously ill, he was so ill we were told to prepare for the worst. We watched your television broadcast often on Sunday mornings because my husband was too ill to go to church. One morning at breakfast I was tearful as I contemplated what it would be like living without him, then suddenly the broadcast came on with you singing, *Don't give up, you're on the brink of a miracle.* With tear-filled eyes I bowed my head and sobbed my way through a simple prayer — thank you Jesus we are on the brink of a miracle. That very week my husband's health picked up, and today he is completely healed."

Whatever God is saying to your heart as you read this, simply obey Him.

Remember, you're on the brink of a miracle. Let's see it happen!

For so many of you who have purchased this book let me leave the words with you and remember …

Don't Give Up You're On The Brink Of A Miracle

Chorus
Don't give up on the brink of a miracle
Don't give in, God is still on the throne
Don't give up on the brink of a miracle
Don't give in, remember you're not alone

Verse One
When satan would have you look
At the trials of life that surround you
And he tries to appear, and bring doubt and fear
All around you
Don't look with the eye, or listen with your ear,
Just cry out to God, He is always near
In your darkest hour, your miracle is here

Verse Two
The devil is a thief, and he sends those troubles
To confound you
And he lies and says 'This time,
There's no way you can find to make it thru'
Remember God's true Word, the battle is the Lord's
Don't give in to fear, think on things that are pure
Praise the Lord, your miracle is here!

Bill Dunn B.A.

CONTACT

To contact Pastor/Evangelist Bill Dunn B.A.
for preaching and singing engagements visit:

www.BillDunn.co.uk
Facebook.com/bill.evangelist
Instagram/BillDunn777

Inspired to write a book?

Contact
Maurice Wylie Media
Your Inspirational Christian Publisher

Based in Northern Ireland and distributing around the world

www.MauriceWylieMedia.com